Understanding Al Qaeda

CW00952195

Understanding Al Qaeda
The Transformation of War

Mohammad-Mahmoud Ould Mohamedou

Pluto Press

LONDON • ANN ARBOR, MI

First published 2007 by Pluto Press
345 Archway Road, London N6 5AA
and 839 Greene Street, Ann Arbor, MI 48106

www.plutobooks.com

British Library Cataloguing in Publication Data
A catalogue record for this book is available from the British Library

ISBN-10   0 7453 2593 9 hardback
ISBN-13   978 0 7453 2593 4 hardback
ISBN-10   0 7453 2592 0 paperback
ISBN-13   978 0 7453 2592 7 paperback

Library of Congress Cataloging in Publication Data applied for

10 9 8 7 6 5 4 3 2 1

Designed and produced for Pluto Press by
Chase Publishing Services Ltd, Fortescue, Sidmouth, EX10 9QG, England
Typeset from disk by Stanford DTP Services, Northampton, England
Printed and bound in Canada by Transcontinental Printing

Contents

List of Figures and Tables

FIGURES

TABLES

Acknowledgements

This book originated with a monograph entitled *Non-Linearity of Engagement: Transnational Armed Groups, International Law, and the War between Al Qaeda and the United States* which I researched and wrote in the first semester of 2005, and which was published by the Program on Humanitarian Policy and Conflict Research (HPCR) at Harvard University. I wish to thank all my colleagues at HPCR for their assistance and encouragement, in particular Claude Bruderlein. The opening chapter expands on an earlier version of an essay entitled 'Responsibility, Injustice, and the American Dilemma', published in the *Buffalo Journal of Human Rights*, which is reworked here with permission, and to which Roger Kaplan, Morris Lipson and Makau Mutua had made greatly appreciated contributions.

George Abi-Saab, Martin Van Creveld, François Burgat and Paul Gilbert offered insightful comments on the argument in Chapter 2 for which I am grateful. I have also benefited from the feedback of faculty and students during lectureships in the autumn of 2005 and winter of 2006 at New York University, the Graduate Institute of Development Studies in Geneva, and the Asser Institute in The Hague. These exchanges allowed me to deepen my thoughts on the questions at hand. A heartfelt thanks to my respective hosts at these institutions, in particular Allen Zerkin, Riccardo Bocco and Avril McDonald. Finally, I would like to record my gratitude to my friend Yves Loffredo for his enduring support and keen understanding of these issues, as well as my appreciation to Roger van Zwanenberg, my editor at Pluto Press, for his support and advice.

I dedicate this work with all my love to my son Kemal and my daughters Bahiya and Zaynab.

'Let me ask you one more thing: can it be that any man has the right to decide about the rest of mankind, who is worthy to live and who is more unworthy?'

'But why bring worth into it? The question is most often decided in the hearts of men not at all on the basis of worth, but for quite different reasons, much more natural ones. As for rights, tell me, who has no right to wish?'

'But surely not for another's death?'

'Maybe even for another's death. Why lie to yourself when everyone lives like that, and perhaps even cannot live any other way?'

Fyodor Dostoevsky, The Brothers Karamazov

Introduction

'The swimmer in the sea does not fear rain'. Thus ends Osama Bin Laden's January 2006 message to the American people, in which he attempts to explain to the citizens of the state he and his group are fighting the reasons for which war is being waged against them. That message was the twentieth since September 2001 when Bin Laden's Al Qaeda had dispatched a group of 19 men to attack military and civilian targets in Washington and New York killing 3,000 Americans. Bin Laden's deputy and second-in-command in Al Qaeda, Ayman al Dhawahiri, had sent 21 other similar messages of his own.

Yet for all their overtness and limpidity – though the formal classical Arabic used by both men translates as awkward, flowery and discursive English – and indeed the English language subtitles embedded in the messages sent after 2004, for most Westerners Al Qaeda's *casus belli* remains murky at best. Re-establishment of the Islamic caliphate, including in Southern Spain, and the conversion of the West to Islam is what most people believe firmly Al Qaeda to be after. Though the organisation has made it clear that it is responding to American policies in the Middle East and has linked consistently three general political demands to cessation of hostilities, peripheral religious references and the group's leaders' religiosity have facilitated the persistence of the invisibilisation of said *casus belli*.

This disappearance – also in part the result of conscious policy choices and the consequence of impatient commentary and scholarship on the question of Al Qaeda – is counterproductive and dangerous. It is particularly surprising that policy-makers and academe choose to ignore the reasons for which a party is going to war, while they substitute justifications of their own ('they hate our way of life', 'they detest democracy and freedom') to those arguments. With the media reporting Qaeda declarations in poorly translated excerpts missing context, the attempted communication is muted. The martial configuration of the conflict can then proceed uninterrupted with an enemy irremediably beyond the pale.

The present book starts with this perceived disconnection between such notional continuity and a practical discontinuity. In helping break through the opacity of the issues, it seeks fundamentally to contribute to remedying the gap between perceptions and realities of the conflict between the United States and Al Qaeda. Those realities include, as well, a context of transformed war wherein the traditional framework depicting international armed conflict is fast proving inadequate in the face of momentous transnational changes.

Chapter 1 sets the issues in context and reviews the historical evolution in which the domestic societal characteristics of the United States have long allowed foreign policy matters to escape reasoned national examination. As the twentieth century closed and as the country's enemies reorganised in novel, unexpected forms, the United States accelerated that blinding sense of exceptionalism. In so doing, America set the stage which enabled maximum exposure for what was objectively a dramatic innovation in international military terms, namely the 11 September 2001 attacks on the World Trade Center and the Pentagon.

That revolutionary transformation, and more generally the changed alchemy of conflict, is the subject of Chapter 2. That section delves into not so much a new conceptualisation of war but rather it seeks to grasp the implications of the new grammar of war grounded in the autonomisation and privatisation of the use of force. Those tectonic changes herald the coming into being of a generation of war and at the same time they echo the warrior ethos of transnational, non-state armed groups that seek to displace the state by conducting war and foreign policy in its stead.

Al Qaeda is the flagship organisation of this mutation playing out before our eyes in the early twenty-first century. Chapter 3 examines the history of the organisation since its creation almost 20 years ago. The different stages through which the entity has gone are depicted and the logic of gradual sophistication and empowerment revealed. In contradistinction to post-11 September analyses doubting the existence of the organisation or arguing that it has merely become a brand name for thousands of faceless international Islamist militants, it is offered that the group has opted consciously for a restructuring whereby a central organ, a mother Al Qaeda (*Al Qaeda al Oum*), is at once coordinating and controlling loosely the actions of semi-independent regional structures around the world.

The nature of the resistances to a scientific, dispassionate understanding of what Al Qaeda is and what it wants is the subject of Chapter 4, which examines briefly the schools of thought arguing the group's irrationality, fundamentalism and hatred. That examination is used to set the stage for Al Qaeda's eminently political animus, one, it is maintained, that is only novel in its configuration. Indeed, the question of terrorism and its understanding as the problematic martial mode used for political purposes by insurgents, rebels, nationalists, separatists and militants since time immemorial remains gnawing. It is so particularly in the case at hand since Al Qaeda has articulated and implemented a strategy in which citizens are held formally accountable for their governments' policies. Such *democratisation of responsibility* is the unexamined mainstay of the war between the United States and Al Qaeda.

Chapter 5 attempts to sketch a way out of the deadlock characterising this conflict, including the remote possibility of some form of negotiations between the two parties. The prevailing reluctance to consider dialogue as a viable option is evaluated against historical precedents pitting state and sub-state groups, and the potential benefits accrued from non-military engagement.

This is a work of political science which borrows from the legal discipline to make a statement relevant to policy-making. It provides an argument about the necessary sober examination of Al Qaeda's *casus belli*. Opposed to the dead end of emotional analysis, culturalist finger-pointing and legalistic dogma, that clinical discussion also entails a scientific re-examination of the nature of the contemporary mode of war and codification of the unconventional means used by newly empowered transnational armed groups such as Al Qaeda.

I
Casus Belli

In spite of all that has been written and said about the 11 September 2001 epoch-changing events and their aftermath, there remains, in the West, a profound reluctance to confront openly the reasons behind the attacks by Al Qaeda on the United States. To many Americans and Europeans, the one question that continues to matter urgently, 'Why did this happen?', remains unanswered satisfactorily. Why *indeed* did this happen? What was driving the perpetrators of the attacks? What made modern, urban-savvy, college-educated young men plan professionally and carefully an operation of this sort? From where did they muster their motivation and dedication? Why were they willing to give their lives in their prime? What reasons stood at the heart of their animus?

Since the attacks were the work of 19 Arab Muslims (15 Saudis, two Emirati, an Egyptian and a Lebanese), the required analysis also concerns the larger relationship between the United States (and, beyond, the West) and the Arabo-Islamic world. These questions cannot, however, be addressed without establishing the historical context in which the events took place.

Catching a nonchalant America engaged more than ever in the business of entertaining itself, the September 2001 attacks on New York and Washington marked the end of American insouciance and closed abruptly the confused decade of transition known as the post-Cold War era. It is in the nature of uncertain times to be defined in relation to what preceded or replaced them, and it is how we may end up remembering the 1990s. In hindsight, those years constituted a decade of chimeras, a make-believe world whose demise was epitomised by the fate of the Oslo Process and the dot.com era. Short-sighted analyses, such as Francis Fukuyama's *End of History* (1992), reigned supported by neo-Orwellian agendas posing as pragmatic accounts of global progress. Fukuyama's approach was thus summarised in his statement that 'for our purposes, it matters very little what strange thoughts occur to people in Albania or Burkina Faso'.[1] As events in the second half of the 1990s started pointing to the persistence of 'real world' problems, and indeed to a 'coming anarchy' in many places around the globe, it became evident that history had not culminated in modern Western liberal democracy and market-oriented capitalism.

The myopic pursuit of that ideal notwithstanding, for most of the twentieth century the United States had been an inspiring land – a nation whose ideals and ways could be and were worthy of admiration worldwide. It was a country that had taken significant steps towards ridding itself of discrimination and class disparities – with uneven success to be certain, but at times with a forceful, nationally shared drive. Though imperfect, its model of democracy was becoming 'the least worst' system that modernity could provide for the West. Gradually, however, American society fell under a spell of cynicism. The ascendancy of greed and of irreverence overtook the land, and – once rationalised – became the measure of all endeavours, leading the country onto a culturally and politically relativist path.

In time, *fin-de-siècle* America had become a voraciously consumerist system with an eager appetite for closure and little patience for complexity. It had evolved into a community characterised by cultural phenomena such as the trivialisation and commodification of everything, the dictate of immediacy and its corollary the end of patience, the individualisation of power, the institutionalisation of cynicism and the infantilisation of people. The cumulative effect of these phenomena was an American oblivious indifference towards the rest of the world. A doctrinaire but somewhat debonair, almost aloof America became engaged in something best described as *démission civilisatrice*, and its self-centredness was tantamount to exclusionary living.

Thereon, such civic cacophony led to an emotional flattening of democracy shoehorned by ignorance of the world, whereas, paradoxically, American culture was reaching the apex of its international influence in the context of globalisation. The anarchy prevailing in the rest of the world – however turbulent, morally arresting and, in cases, resulting partly from US foreign policy – could not be allowed to disturb the national appraisal of prosperity.

A manufactured perception of peace was forced on international events. Such denial produced a numbing of the political senses. In the United States, this endured until the bourgeois and commercial passions for material well-being were shaken to their foundations on 11 September 2001, and the urgent need for a cultural market correction was provided by Al Qaeda's attack on the American homeland. A nation bloated by good living realised suddenly that it had serious enemies, which it had dismissed dangerously in a blind fit of ethnocentrism.

When not unreflective about the world around it, America had indeed oftentimes been antagonistic towards large parts of it. The enmity of the United States was nowhere more manifested than in its relationship with Islam (as a faith) and Arabs (as a people). The unprecedented economic prosperity and the global political power that the United States had enjoyed in the 1990s were linked to the end of the Cold War, but also, and possibly more directly, to the outcome of the 1990–91 Gulf War. The selling of that unfinished conflict as a political and military success combined with the euphoria of having drawn back safely from the brink of World War III to set the stage for a period where Americans (and later Europeans and Third World elites) would indeed want to focus exclusively on 'the economy, stupid'. In addition, the CNN-delivered portrayal of a 'heroic' American army helped cure the psychological trauma of the Vietnam war, and endow (temporarily) America with self-confidence. The decade that followed was in significant measure about the blowback of that war, which would only be settled decisively on 9 April 2003 with the fall of the Ba'ath regime in Baghdad.

Contrary to what many believe, the September 2001 attacks did not mark the opening salvo of the contest between the United States and Al Qaeda. To adduce this claim is to ignore that the long-coddled conflict had been going on for a while, and that 11 September was merely escalation of a pattern that had begun following the 1990–91 Gulf War. On 21 January 1996, the *New York Times* featured a self-explanatory lead story entitled 'Seeing Green: The Red Menace Is Gone. But Here's Islam', which constituted a sign of things to come after 2001.

Between 1991 and 2001, America sustained, as it were, six major assaults by Al Qaeda: the 26 February 1993 first World Trade Center operation; the 13 November 1995 bombing of a Saudi-American base in Riyadh; the 25 June 1996 attack on the Al Khobar towers near Dhahran, Saudi Arabia (housing site for the crews enforcing the no-fly zones over Iraq); the simultaneous bombings of the US embassies in Kenya and Tanzania on 7 August 1998; the attack against the USS *Cole* warship in Yemen on 12 October 2000; and the operation against the World Trade Center and the Pentagon on 11 September 2001. In addition, there had been at least two thwarted attacks: a plot to explode eleven American airliners over the Pacific Ocean in January 1995, and in December 2000 a bombing (possibly of the Space Needle) during the millennial festivities in Seattle, Washington.

For its part, the US government had been consistently and increasingly in conflict with Muslims and Arabs. According to the US Defense Department, between 1980 and 1995 the United States engaged in 17 military operations in the Middle East, every one of them directed against Muslims. The United States also took direct action against Muslims in Iraq throughout the 1990s, and in the Sudan and Afghanistan on 20 August 1998. No such pattern – which multiplied dramatically in the years that followed, culminating in the war in Iraq – occurred against the people of any other civilisation.[2] US hegemonic attitudes towards the Islamic world and America's failure to recognise the violent resentment that its policies were nourishing further fuelled the conflict, setting the stage for 11 September.

THE SERIOUSNESS OF INJUSTICE

With the veil of ignorance lifted abruptly, post-September 2001 Americans began asking themselves all kinds of questions with despondency. Looking contentedly on the order of things – 1990s style – was no longer an option as interrogations abounded. Could the United States remain a superpower? Should it embrace empire-making? Should it resort to torture? How was it to handle a new type of war for which it was not prepared? Who are the Arabs? What is Islam?

Cut adrift by the shattering of their reality, Americans could not cushion the emotional experience. The sense of disconnectedness was too powerful. Yet though there could have been no bigger wake up call than the events that transpired on 11 September, it was as if nothing was learned. The central reasons behind the sociogenesis of the attacks remained unnamed. The Gulf War matrix was dusted off. 'Osama' joined and dethroned 'Saddam' in the pantheon of all-star villains (though Hussein continued to run a close second) and, ten years later, Arabs were again an obscure enemy.

The replacement answers provided by officials and commentators alike – 'they hate our way of life',[3] 'they detest democracy', 'this is a war of freedom-loving people against evil barbarians' – were equally misleading. For far too long, Americans had been listening complacently to analysts who contributed actively to their cecity towards the political grievances of more than a billion individuals. No stranger blindness indeed than the one of a democratic country fuelled by a devotion to Israel that knows no satiety and that cancels all reasoned thinking.[4] The result of such stigmatising discourse and dichotomising history was that, as Don DeLillo remarked, the sense of disarticulation heard in the formula 'Us versus Them' had never been so striking, at either end.[5]

Amid this flotsam and jetsam, questions were asked about who had done this and how come it could have happened, but there were no proper introspections into why the 2001 attacks took place. While the answer to it is quite clear to Arabs and Muslims around the world, as noted, the question that remains unanswered to many an American is 'Why did this happen?' In fact, proper inquiry into the reasons behind the events has come to be regarded as almost insidious. The late Edward Said pointed out that

> the least likely argument to be listened to in the United States in the public domain is one that suggests that there are historical reasons why America, as a major world actor, has drawn such animosity to itself by virtue of what it has done ... The assumption seems to be that ... any minimizing or explanation of that is an intolerable idea even to contemplate, much less to investigate rationally.[6]

Why then did Osama Bin Laden's Al Qaeda attack the United States in September 2001? Mainly, the answer is a deep and heavy sense of injustice harboured by a transnational armed group self-championing the feelings of millions around the Arab and Islamic world. The issue is not Islamic fundamentalism, religious fanaticism, poverty or the lack of democracy in the Arab world. It is justice and the yearning for it. Specifically, the perception of American injustice displayed as the unceasing and unflinching support for Israel's occupation of Palestinian territories, the continued assistance to authoritarian Arab regimes, and the expanded US military presence in the Middle East. It bears reminding that it is not America's paramountcy that is resented, but its hegemonic policies. The predominance is an accepted fact to most Muslims.

Many in the United States and some in Europe have argued that those who committed the attacks 'hate our way of life'. These protests are hypocritical. Few Arabs hate the West's way of life to the point of committing kamikaze attacks, but a far larger number of Muslim youth – who need not be dim-witted lunatics – resent America's policies and its *pax Americana* in the Middle East. With the American and British colonisation of Iraq, this feeling is set to multiply in the years ahead. As evidenced by America's own reply to the September 2001 attacks, revenge is a powerful motivation and victimhood is no myth – it is a painful reality to large numbers of dispossessed Arabs and Muslims, including the families of the thousands killed in Iraq. Yet for many an American it is difficult to countenance the fact that there might be more to the 11 September operation or the Iraqi resistance than religious fanaticism or terrorism, namely a political dimension.

Post-11 September 2001 civil liberties clamp downs have been rationalised similarly by several American commentators. Michelle Malkin writes, for instance, that 'racial profiling – or more precisely, threat profiling – is justified'.[7] Statements such as those of nationally syndicated columnist Ann Coulter who opined that 'we should invade their countries, kill their leaders, and convert them to Christianity', or former Italian Prime Minister Silvio Berlusconi's claim, on 28 September 2001, that Western civilisation is 'superior' to the Islamic one, or Reverend Jerry Falwell's 6 October 2002 remark that the Prophet Mohammad is 'a terrorist', or indeed President George W. Bush's 15 September 2001 declaration that 'this crusade ... is going to take a while' attest to the fact that reactions to the 11 September attacks were often along civilisational lines. Such hatred – awakened at once and embodied in Italian journalist Orianna Fallaci's diatribe-filled bestseller *The Rage and the Pride* (2002) – is also what made it easy for many a Westerner to, overnight, start seeing Osama Bin Laden (previously a supporting character in the background noise of world politics) as the new face of evil, rather than considering soberly the reasons he and those he leads elected war.

MISREPRESENTATIONS AND DISTORTIONS

Not asking the right societal questions – Have we been committing injustice? Should we reassess our foreign policy? Are these choices worth the price paid? – the United States could hardly come up with the proper political answers. This has led the 'land of the free' on a path where, within months, institutionalised racism became tolerated nationwide, torture was rationalised,[8] and the very same indoctrination methods that characterise dictatorial regimes, including secret trials, ghost detainees, secret prisons, self-censorship and witch-hunts, were implemented nationwide. By 2002, sweeping legislation introduced secretly had departed radically from the constitutional guarantees at the core of American democracy: the rights to an independent judiciary, trial by jury, public proceedings, due process, *habeas corpus* and appeals to higher courts. In time, the country embarked on an illegal, immoral and ill-advised colonial war on a sovereign state.

If the United States of the late 1990s was a country yearning for meaning, post-11 September America ached for direction. It knew only too well and, for most, merely intuitively, that something about its behaviour was amiss, but – 'militarist, agitated, uncertain, anxious, projecting its internal disorder on the planet'[9] – it refused to admit this bifurcation. The self-congratulating masquerade that was displayed in full effect after September 2001 was no recipe for responsible leadership in the face of national tragedy. Almost in all matters, America's reply – including that of the majority of its intellectuals[10] – took the form of a martialist reasserting of American imperialism, disguised as legitimate, defensive patriotism, rather than a re-examining and reassessing of its problematic policies. This was clearly the adobe of the Bush administration's 2002 *National Security Strategy*, which redefined the country's approach to international politics along lines that rested on the use of imperial phraseology: 'We will disrupt and destroy', 'We will … wage a war'.

More dangerously for Americans, the United States government did not hesitate to change its laws to non-democratic ones to dispose of its foreign and domestic enemies. Similarly, the mainstream American media have, for the most, foregone their information mission, namely to report the facts objectively and dispassionately, and any dissenting views were denounced, often by respected national commentators, as unpatriotic and treasonous.

One of the few leading dissenting voices, Norman Mailer remarked that, after 11 September 2001, Americans took a shock that was not wholly out of proportion to what happened to the Germans after World War I, and that this blow to their sense of security allowed a form of fascism to creep in whereby the United States could become a species of totalitarian country, dominating the world, with very little freedom of speech.[11] Interestingly, it is novelists more than intellectuals who have been the most vocal and openly critical about the post-9/11 dangers of US policies. Others, like human rights activists, who have documented and denounced generically the undemocratic nature of the counter-terrorist measures adopted, have seldom addressed the larger picture of the meaning of such drift for America, at home and abroad.

For the first time since the US government's mistreatment of Japanese nationals and descendants in the 1940s, civil liberties and freedoms were curbed officially. Particularly alarming was the upsurge of xenophobia. In a 16 September 2001 *USA Today*/CNN/Gallup poll asking Americans their reactions to the attacks in New York and Washington, 49 per cent of the interviewees said that they would approve requiring Arabs, including those who were US citizens, to carry a special identity card; 58 per cent were in favour of requiring Arabs, including those who were US citizens, to undergo special, more intensive security checks before boarding airplanes in the United States. This Yellow Star-like hysteria reached the point where the credentials of a US Secret Service agent of Arab lineage entrusted with protecting the American President were questioned by a flight attendant and the agent was unceremoniously deboarded off a commercial flight.

Axiologically, the simplistic gung-ho, in-your-face approach of the George W. Bush administration catered to feelings of punishment rather than the idea of justice. The go get'em demagogy led to the dehumanisation of the enemy, setting the stage for its 'eradication' and (sexual and religious) humiliation. As one analyst aptly notes, the elephant in the room that nobody wants to acknowledge in the 11 September–Afghanistan–Iraq debate is conquest: '[O]ld fashioned conquest, in which ground is seized and populations controlled against their will for extended periods'.[12] Consequently, the previously unseen and unknown Muslims became the subject and object of Western paranoia and justice had to be *brought* to them – courtesy of Star Wars' Stormtroopers-looking US soldiers roaming the planet in search of Muslim 'rebels' – in Afghanistan, Iraq, Pakistan, Yemen, the Sahel and elsewhere.

In that context, whether one admits it or not, concepts such as 'the West' and 'Islam' carry weight and meaning. More importantly, they summon loyalty – today possibly more than ever in recent history. Yet the conventional Western public discourse does not accommodate constructively such clarity of vision. It uses cultural reference only to reinforce oft-repeated notions such as the idea that Islam is the one major world culture that has 'problems' with modernity, imposing in effect a subjective universality. Scorned, Islam is presented as intolerant and antimodern – it has 'a problem'.[13]

For a long time, the West tended to be dismissive and contemptuous of Islamists, who were regarded, by security specialists no less, as powerless lunatics. Indulging such clichés and dismissing its enemies so easily blinded Americans domestically and reinforced the perception of an arrogant America abroad. The codification of this practice was enabled by a vast literature purporting to 'explain' Arab politics through the tokenistic understanding of an alleged idiosyncratic Arab psychology. The founding texts of that tradition had been Raphael Patai's *The Arab Mind* (1973) and David Pryce-Jones' *The Closed Circle: An Interpretation of the Arabs* (1989). After 11 September, the trend became almost openly racist and expanded to encompass all Muslims.

Yet, in the face of so much planning and meticulous preparation, it defies logic that the 11 September team was anything less than a professional commando dispatched by a powerful and elite leadership. Mohammad Atta had earned a *summa cum laude* PhD, Ziad Jarrah was fluent in four languages, Ayman al Dhawahiri[14] is a surgeon and Osama Bin Laden is a millionaire.

Similarly, locating the causes of Al Qaeda's resort to force in the fermentation of contemporary Islamic culture, rather than in the militarisation of the politics of a sub-state armed group with international ambitions, was short-sighted. The oft-heard argument that it is the failure of Arab societies to develop democracy in their midst that breeds foreign terrorism is equally misleading. Though the state–society relationship in all of the Arab countries had traditionally been, at best, a rocky one, democratisation was initiated and gained momentum in the early 1990s in some countries where serious attempts at developing and retaining a degree of independence on the part of the civil society took place. Nevertheless, this population had to face the challenge of an alternative project of society put forth by Islamist groups, at the same time that it found itself battling the existing authoritarian regimes and their resistance to change. Eventually, buttressed by the repressive behaviour of the regimes and the historical legacy of ill-advised secularisation experiences, a politicised Islam of rebellion emerged on an order of magnitude beyond the region. As it were, the countries that had demonstrated the greatest willingness to distance themselves from a religiously organised political system (Algeria, Tunisia, Syria and Egypt) came to be the ones where Islamist activity had become the most prominent.

Although the long-term nature of this evolution is necessarily indeterminate, an assessment of the state of human liberties and political freedom in the region indicates that the resentment is essentially domestic. The demands and activism are mostly, and in some cases exclusively, directed locally towards the repressive regimes, such as Mubarak's Egypt, the Saud's Saudi Arabia, Ben Ali's Tunisia, Bouteflika's Algeria and King Abdullah's Jordan – all of which are steadfast US allies.

Consequently, it can be maintained that had the 22 Arab countries been fully-fledged democracies, the attacks of September 2001 could have still taken place. The reason is that the issues that mobilised Mohammad Atta, and which continue to motivate Osama Bin Laden and Ayman al Dhawahiri, were eminently political, and about justice and power asymmetry, not about the local struggles for political liberalisation.

In a televised message to the American people, broadcast by Al Jazeera on 29 October 2004, Osama Bin Laden explained that the best way for Americans to avoid a repeat of the 11 September 2001 attacks was to stop threatening Muslims' security:

> It had not occurred to our mind to attack the [twin] towers, but after our patience ran out and we saw the injustice and the inflexibility of the American–Israeli alliance towards our people in Palestine and Lebanon, this came to my mind. As I watched the destroyed towers in Lebanon, it occurred to me to punish the unjust the same way – to destroy towers in America so that it can taste some of what we are tasting and stop killing our children and women.[15]

A little more than a year later, on 19 January 2006, Bin Laden extended an offer of truce to the United States grounded in 'fair conditions'. Three months later, in a 23 April message, he considered that his offer had been rejected and the American people were willing to continue supporting their government's war effort.

In the final aesthetic, for the new breed of kamikazes represented by Al Qaeda, the dual source of armed action is the question of political injustice and territorial dispossession. Their war-making potential is anchored in their ability to disrupt and paralyse their enemy through constant reminders of their indefatigability. In the event, the combined failure and emasculation of post-colonial and recolonised states has led to a democratisation and privatisation of the struggle against foreign domination – ushering the international rise of non-state actors filling the power vacuum with demonstrated military ambitions.

2
Changed Context

> We must then pursue our efforts, however painful, to drive war everywhere without giving the Arabs time to breathe. We must go in all directions so as to surprise them, dazzle them and show them that devastation no longer follows the straight lines forecasted.
>
> Alexis de Tocqueville[1]

In the wake of the 11 September 2001 attacks on New York and Washington, a uniform discourse emerged as regards the nature of the war pitting the United States government against the transnational armed Islamist group known as Al Qaeda. This dominant perspective presented the fundamental parameters of the conflict as an open-and-shut matter of good versus evil. Several years after the battle was joined fully and almost a decade since hostilities were declared formally, no elements of twilight have materialised. Dogmatic scholarship and trenchant practice continue to depict non-military engagement with Al Qaeda as improper and unnecessary. Eradication – the preferred approach of French colonial authorities in 1950s Algeria and Algeria's authoritarian government fighting Islamist militants in the 1990s – is the dominant approach. Via this autopsy, revelation of the purpose and structure of Al Qaeda are crudely mechanistic.

The results of this struggle of epochal significance – which has come to be known misleadingly as a 'war on terror' – cannot be overstated. In less than five years, the world order has been reshaped and paradigmatic shifts introduced in the constituent parts of the international system, now through the adversaries' avowed actions, now by way of their antagonistic interaction.

Set standards of international law have come under attack at a *staccato* pace even before being achieved fully.

Among the key unresolved factual, legal and policy questions, the nature of the war waged by Al Qaeda remains, paradoxically, misunderstood. Marked by a persistent failure to try and understand, the majority of analyses within academe and journalism have been ideological. Overwhelmingly, the issues are not spoken of in an objective, scientific mode. Alongside the conspicuous absence of a precise *topos* and the proliferation of dichotomous analyses, reification of one of the belligerents is linked intimately to its vilification. A central contradiction of this discourse is that Al Qaeda is presented simultaneously as a terrorist group that must be apprehended and a new entity that calls for special measures and novel categories (e.g., 'illegal combatants').

Such undifferentiated understanding and rejection of the cogency of Al Qaeda's war are, however, but transitive phenomena. The group's wherewithal and the nature of the contest are calling for a reassessment of the basic categories at hand. To wit, empirical inquiry and historical exactitude indicate that Al Qaeda's is a formulation hitherto unknown, essentially the result of a natural cumulative evolution and an insistent logic of discourse and practice.

Al Qaeda is an industrious, committed and power-wielding versatile organisation exerting an extraordinary amount of influence and waging a political, limited and evasive war of attrition – not a religious, open-ended, apocalyptic one. In the space of ten years (1996–2006), Al Qaeda has implemented a clearly articulated policy, skilfully conducted several complex military operations, and demonstrated strategic operational flexibility. Of late, this unprecedented transnational phenomenon has exhibited an ability to operate successfully and innovatively amid heightened and widespread international counter-measures.

To be certain, the novelty of the role played by Al Qaeda has been stated resoundingly. Yet it has not been fully understood, debated and analysed with a view to inform an international policy and legal process wherein imperial hyper-power begat rebellious hyper-resistance. The cumulative effect of these complex, ongoing processes has generated a situation where, in particular, satisfactory explanations of the question of causation remain elusive. The literature is dominated by exegesis narratives flavoured with hostility and ungainly repetition. To subject, therefore, Al Qaeda to rational analysis and consider creatively its principled political action and symmetrical compulsion is needed urgently.

CLASSICAL WAR

The end of the twentieth century was marked by a gradual breakdown in international rules governing the use of force. With all its violence and potential for nuclear war, the Cold War had the virtue of controlling the flow of violence.[2] It represented a visible edifice of antinomian forces whose waning led, in particular, to a transformation in the way conflict is channelled, conducted and justified.

> At the beginning of the Cold War, that regime stressed the inviolability of obligations in accordance with the norm *pacta sunt servanda* (treaties are binding). By the last decade of that conflict, there was increased support for the legal doctrine of *rebus sic stantibus*, which terminated agreements if the circumstances at the time of the signing no longer obtained.[3]

In time, cavalier attitudes to law, dismissal of agreements, treaties and institutions, as well as the selective application of the law, and a general recklessness with consensus-based international projects, underscored an absence of accountability and undermining of the rule of law.

These vistas of thinking ushered a period propitious to the rise of a multicentric, interdependent world with emancipated transnational actors. The previously stalemated international scene was transforming. A shift to a new paradigm, whose basic assumptions were that if state practice could be modified so could sub-state practice, occurred with a dialectical synthesis subsuming previous forms of disintegrative actions. In that context, Al Qaeda was born following a modern systemic principle of political and militaristic organisation.

Ensuingly, the world emerged from the immediate post-9/11 period and the wars in Afghanistan and Iraq only to enter the longer term, historical post-11 September era, the characteristics of which are fourfold: the transformation of the temporal and spatial elements of conflict, the mutation of the belligerents' identity, the expansion of the nature of targets (now encompassing political, social and cultural symbols), and the systematisation of privatised asymmetrical warfare (expressed on the mode 'my security depends on the insecurity that I can inflict upon you').

The type of war that had come to be recognised as archetypal – simultaneous and orderly, symmetrical interstate conflict – had crystallised over time and was, arguably, merely a step in an ongoing evolution. The gradual development and implementation of the *ius belli* had led, well before the 1949 Geneva Conventions, to the establishment of an architecture whereby practices considered 'cruel and unnecessary' had been banned from interstate armed conflict. In time, a framework delineating obligations and awarding rights in a predictable manner was organised precisely. The consequential shift concerned conceptions of law in terms of what was to be regarded as permissible and impermissible militarily. Arbitrary abuses were no longer to be tolerated on the battlefield.

Over recent centuries, the grammar of war has, in effect, undergone four generational changes. Following the Middle Ages, a first generation, which dominated during the large-scale Napoleonic wars of the late 1700s and early 1800s, was concerned with massed manpower (with soldiers fighting shoulder to shoulder) and was driven by the destruction of the enemy's close force. The second generation, illustrated by the stalemated trench warfare of World War I, was aimed at the destruction of the enemy's fighting force and focused therefore on massed firepower (e.g., the long-barrelled field guns Howitzer and 'Big Bertha'). A third period placed emphasis on the destruction of the enemy's command and control and was characterised, consequently, by the importance of strategic manoeuvring. The tactical advantage granted by that latter innovation was best encapsulated during World War II with the engagements pitting mobile German mechanised units against fixed French troops positioned behind the Maginot Line.

Regardless of their respective foci (manpower, firepower or mobility), these three generations operated within a common traditional war paradigm that had three key characteristics: war was a relationship between men as soldiers, armed conflict took place between states, and states enjoyed the monopoly of organised violence. This normative construct had crystallised over two centuries and was captured notably in the writings of Jean-Jacques Rousseau (*The Social Contract*, 1762), Karl Von Clausewitz (*On War*, 1832), and Max Weber (*The Theory of Social and Economic Organisation*, 1915).

The classic conflict paradigm was characterised in particular by a static spatio-temporal configuration and by group differentiation. War took place, as the phrase went, at 'the appointed hour of battle', and it was the affair of soldiers (and, sometimes, mercenaries). Civilians, defined negatively as non-combatants, stood by the wayside and were no longer to be harmed. The consecration of this configuration of the character of conflict was primarily the result of an evolution influenced by the regularisation of the function of soldiery. Such delineation – underscored by geographic and demographic expansion which called for further regulation of military corps – came to operate on the necessary correlation between technological and legal precision. In other words, if armies were to come to clash at an agreed time and place, with known types of actors licensed to kill, then rules had to be devised precisely and followed at least minimally.

WESTERN WAR, WESTERN LAW

The standard-setting efforts that were under way during the nineteenth century mostly concerned powerful European nations. Thus, definition and codification of international law were initially unilateral and exclusionary. If, per the newly established rules of war, objects of attack were to be limited eventually to military targets, round the world, colonised civilians subject to European rule (and their assets) would continue to be attacked indiscriminately well into the twentieth century.

The political economy of violence and the synchronic evolution in the institutionalisation of the principle of distinction between combatants and non-combatants were indeed, for a long time and until quite recently, paralleled by a policy of indistinction in relation to wars conducted by European powers in their colonies. At the very same time that diplomatic conferences were held in Europe – Geneva (1863), Brussels (1874), The Hague (1899 and 1907), London (1909) – to agree humane, professional and civilised ways to conduct warfare and avoid unnecessary suffering in the prosecution of international armed conflict, a number of the states gathered therein were involved in conflicts in Africa, the Middle East and Asia in which targeting of civilian populations was tolerated and often planned for as part of 'necessary' security measures. Witness, for instance, the campaigns of the British in Kenya, the French in Algeria, the Belgians in the Congo and the Germans in South West Africa.

Policies underscored by the modern understanding that technical superiority provides a natural right to annihilate the enemy even when he is defenceless[4] and by a logic of militarisation of particular populations were often surprisingly historically contemporaneous of the very codification of international humanitarian law.

By the beginning of the twentieth century, it was European habit to distinguish between civilised wars and colonial wars. The laws of war applied to wars among the civilised nation-states, but the laws of nature were said to apply to colonial wars, and the extermination of the lower races was seen as a biological necessity.[5]

In French-ruled Algeria (1830–1962), for instance,

war became total ... with Algerian populations regarded as non-conventional enemies that could and had to be annihilated in some circumstances ... [Their] territories were considered military objectives, which implied the disappearance of any sanctuary to escape from the violence of battles. This evolution had as a consequence the massive destruction of cities, villages and cultures.[6]

Such emblematic binary coding – encapsulated in German historian Heinrich Von Treitschke's statement that 'international law becomes phrases if its standards are also applied to barbaric people'[7] – persisted well into the second half of the twentieth century, in effect informing the strategy adopted, for instance, by French political authorities during the 1950s and early 1960s. As Olivier Le Cour Grandmaison notes:

> During the recent [Algerian] conflict, in 1954, practices used regularly during the conquest were resorted to anew and perfected in a context where the 'necessities' of combat against 'terrorists' justified the recourse to non-conventional means such as mass torture, collective reprisals against civilians, summary executions, destroying of villages, and the forced displacement of Algerian populations in camps set up by the military. Remarkable permanence of total war.[8]

Such continuity has indeed been a sporadic feature of transgressions on the part of the military, leading some to argue that 'the Western way of war is so lethal precisely because it is so amoral – shackled rarely by concerns of ritual, tradition, religion, or ethics, by anything other than military necessity'.[9] In 1956, Paris Police Chief Maurice Papon was declaring that 'the hour is no longer one of distinction between civilians and the military', adding, a year later: 'I ask all civilians to behave as soldiers ... there is no longer "soldiers" and "civilians" ... there must only be soldiers'.[10]

Even today, the majority of analyses of war remain US- and Euro-centric in character, inclined to take the Western state as a norm, and likely to focus on technological triumphalism.[11] It is indeed important to note that, much as the contemporary rules of war were developed out of the congress of nineteenth- and twentieth-century European powers, thus reflecting the *duellum* dynamics that these countries were concerned with, recent re-examinations of warfare and its codification have tended similarly to be United States- and Europe-centric. If both states of affairs reflect, first and foremost, the power of these actors, their concern with war, as well as their ability to project their might internationally, such understanding necessarily omits a host of other actors whose approach to war often differs radically from the Western canon.

An important recent exception to the domination of Western-centred texts on war, and a harbinger of the current metamorphosis of conflict was provided in 1999 by two Chinese military officers, Qiao Liang and Wang Xiangsui, in a book entitled *Unrestricted Warfare*, in which the authors remarked that 'from this point on, war will no longer be what it was originally … It can no longer be carried out in the ways with which we are familiar … The metamorphosis of war will have a more complex backdrop'. Liang and Xiangsui also argued that 'the first rule of unrestricted warfare is that there are no rules'.[12] These two dimensions, the fundamental reassessment of the categories used to depict conflict and the radical transformation of the mechanics of war, constitute the basic ingredients of the new wars.

BELLUM NOVAE

The classic war paradigm was characterised by five predominant features that enabled its uniformisation and functioning: *monopoly* (of the use of force, of legitimacy), *distinction* (between civil and military, between legitimate and illegitimate warriors, between internal and external, and between public and private), *concentration* (of forces, of targeted sectors), *brevity* (of conception, of battle) and *linearity* (of organisation, of engagement).

Organisationally, the last two dimensions were key framing principles. As early as the Lieber Code, drafted by Francis Lieber in 1863 at the request of President Abraham Lincoln, it was offered, in Article 29, that '[t]he more vigorously wars are pursued, the better it is for humanity. Sharp wars are brief'. This precept was to remain a constant in military planning of wars, displayed consistently in the German doctrine of *Blitzkrieg* and, more recently, in the American doctrine of 'Rapid Dominance', commonly known as 'Shock and Awe'.[13] Linearity, for its part, was also enacted through the loss of autonomy of soldiers. Almost overnight confined to barracks, integrated into variegated and specialised corps, troops became controlled, supervised and provided for by bureaucratic organisations.

Further, this arrangement of linearity and brevity could be seen to play out universally. For instance, within the traditional Bedouin setting in the Middle East and North Africa, classical war was conceived of similarly as a linear matter of decisive 'here and now' encounters. As Robert Montagne notes:

> The usual manner to engage combat was to mobilise tribes on both sides and to align its forces. Camels were sat along two parallel lines ... Combatants would then engage in incessant, day-long singular combats between the two lines ... The affair ... end[ed] with a general charge and the ruin of one of the sides.[14]

Yet, inevitably, the configuration of conflict evolves overtime. The end of the twentieth century and the beginning of the twenty-first witnessed the downgrading of Westphalian symmetrical conflict and the birth of a fourth generation of war. Whereas the previous three generations focused respectively on gathered manpower, assembled firepower and decisive manoeuvring, this latest generation is concerned centrally with the destruction of the enemy's political will to fight and is, thus, characterised by the notion of network warfare.

The fourth generation of war corresponds additionally to the waxing of a new war paradigm defined mostly by a two-pronged phenomenon: the diminishing of intra-state war and the appearance of new patterns of international war, namely between states and transnational armed groups. In this mutated alchemy of conflict, states have lost the monopoly of war, and free and powerful self-forming infra-state agents are interjecting themselves across spatial and temporal boundaries.

To be certain, the conceptual and practical replacement is not absolute – seldom do international affairs paradigms shift so completely – but the evolution does represent a definite change and a reframing illustrated by a lengthy and tested alteration of the system's matrix, namely an autonomisation of forms of violence.

Another important characteristic of the transformations underscoring the most recent generation change, and in particular its key feature, the rise of transnationalism, is de-statisation. States are losing ground and power primarily because they no longer enjoy monopoly over the use of force. Mary Kaldor captured the idea of eroding monopolisation thus:

> The new wars arise in the context of the erosion of the autonomy of the state and in some extreme cases the disintegration of the state. In particular, they occur in the context of the erosion of the monopoly of legitimate organised violence. This monopoly is eroded from above and from below. It has been eroded from above by the transnationalisation of military forces which began during the two world wars and was institutionalised by the bloc system during the Cold War and by innumerable transnational connections between armed forces that developed in the post-war period.[15]

Didier Bigo argues that de-statisation began as early as the eighteenth century, and that the reason the Westphalian system functioned for so long is that it had succeeded in establishing a circular logic whereby contestation of the state had to pass through the state itself, thus inviting further state intervention. Calling for an understanding of conflictuality independently of the state, he notes that the essentialist categories used to analyse the state – sovereignty, law – are not merely objective categories of political science, but, as it were, are tools in the hands of the state.[16]

Finally, recent conflicts have featured an eroding distinction between participants. As noted, the legal precepts that had evolved in the course of the nineteenth and twentieth centuries were aimed at de-civilianisation of the battlefield. With the loss of control by the state of the formal use of force, civilians have increasingly found themselves involved directly in the new wars. Even before the current wave of transnationality, 'total war', as exemplified by particular campaigns during World War II and the 1950–60s wars of liberation, had diluted significantly the formal notions of distinction.

Table 2.1   Traditional Conflict Paradigm

Specific moment and place
Encounter on a battlefield

Sharply etched sequential timeframe
Recognisable beginning and end of engagement

Well-defined actors
Soldiers (as state agents), civilians

Armies attacking armies
Military targets, siege warfare, proportionality

Traditional weaponry
Targeted used of kinetic force

The new transformations took place, in particular, in the context of the aftermath of the attacks launched by Al Qaeda on 11 September 2001 on the United States. For all practical purposes, the new war paradigm is, in effect, embodied and at the same time furthered by Al Qaeda. Initially, however, the nature of the conflict being simultaneously born and revealed in New York and Washington was obscure, thus allowing an acrimonious sense of exceptionalism and derogation to appear. In simple terms, two schools came to offer different answers to the question of whether international humanitarian law was relevant to the 'war on terror'. While one argued that the world had changed, that there was a new architecture limiting the application of the Geneva Conventions, another maintained that large-scale terrorism was nothing novel, and that greater magnitude did not imply necessarily a shift of paradigm.

Admittedly limited and possibly a rule-proving anomaly, Al Qaeda's exceptionalism indicates, nevertheless, a genuine departure from the existing state-centred conflict format. What is more, in the case of Al Qaeda, such insurrectionary war is thought out, enacted and commented upon in a conscious and forward-looking manner by the actor itself. In essence, transnational armed groups of this type are questioning the primacy of the state by highlighting how the traditional, exclusive and self-evident determination of international law is problematic.

Turning its tactical deficiency into a strategic advantage, Al Qaeda has been operating, too, in a radically transformed context:

> [The] strategic redefinition of the instruments and locations of war reached its provisional peak on 11 September 2001 ... The conversion of formerly subordinate tactical elements into an independent strategy therefore rests upon a major extension of the fields of conflict and a fundamental redefinition of the instruments of force. The monopoly on the means of war enjoyed by the armed forces, which was typical of Europe from the seventeenth to the twentieth century, is now a thing of the past.[17]

Against such historical background, the current conflict between Al Qaeda and the United States illustrates vividly the evolution of warfare in three respects. First, a non-state actor party to an international conflict is positioning itself functionally and consciously on different planes of the power continuum. This has implied the expansion of the panoply of means at the disposition of Al Qaeda; not merely terrorism but the full range of kinetic force to influence its enemy. In an effort to compensate for the disparity in logistical military capability, the sub-state actor has sought to expand the platform of combat. Disparity is no deterrent, inasmuch as it is no longer functioning on a straightforward plane of quantitative advantage. The nature and quality of attacks balance that lack of equilibrium.

Such new generation of warfare is referred to as asymmetric:

> In broad terms, [it is] likely to be widely dispersed and largely undefined; the distinction between war and peace will be blurred to the vanishing point. It will be non-linear, possibly to the point of having no definable battlefields or fronts. The distinction between 'civilian' and 'military' may

disappear. Actions will occur concurrently throughout all participants' depth, including their society as a cultural, not just a physical, entity.[18]

Asymmetry spells a disinclination to prosecute wars swiftly – which, as noted, has been the preferred approach of states from *Blitzkrieg* to 'Shock and Awe'. It entails, in particular, a systematic deceleration of the use of force on the part of the non-state armed group. As Herfried Münkler notes,

> asymmetrical warfare, the salient feature of the new wars in recent decades, is based to a large extent on the different velocities at which the parties wage war on each other: asymmetries of strength are based on a capacity for acceleration which outstrips that of the enemy, whereas asymmetries of weakness are based on a readiness and ability to slow down the pace of war.[19]

The point deserves emphasis that, as a compensatory means of warfare, non-linearity of engagement serves principally to detach the transnational non-state group from vulnerability and permanent exposure to its more powerful, lawful government enemy. Secondarily, non-linearity offsets – rather than outpaces – the state's calibration of its use of force. In that way, asymmetry is no longer merely a condition but becomes a full-blown strategy.

Al Qaeda has opted consciously for a different usage of the notion of time than its state opponent(s). It has instrumentalised the temporal dimension in two respects. On the one hand, whereas its enemies pursue swiftness, the organisation seeks to prolong the conflict. On the other, by extending the engagement, the group enables itself to strike when it is ready while keeping its enemy constantly in a protracted state of defensive anticipation. To a large extent, this version of war is a throwback to a Hobbesian configuration:

> For war consisteth not in battle only, or the act of fighting, but in a tract of time, wherein the will to contend by battle is sufficiently known: and therefore the notion of time is to be considered in the nature of war, as it is in the nature of weather. For as the nature of foul weather lieth not

in a shower or two of rain, but in an inclination thereto of many days together: so the nature of war consisteth not in actual fighting, but in the known disposition thereto during all the time there is no assurance to the contrary.[20]

Table 2.2   New Conflict Paradigm

Enlargement of the spatial dimension
Geographical indeterminacy of theatre of operations

Transformation of the temporal element
Simultaneous multiplicity of points of interaction; concurrent acceleration and deceleration of engagement

Mutation of the belligerents' identity
Obliteration of combatant/civilian categories

Expansion of the nature of targets
Increasing blending of civilian and military targets

Systematisation of asymmetrical warfare
Amplification of the platform of combat; weaponisation of civilian assets

---

The second consequential shift of this new type of conflict is that a non-state armed group whose members belong to several countries has declared war on a few states and their citizens, regarding war as a punishment for what can be termed 'privatised collective responsibility'. According to this argument, civilians are considered to be involved tangentially in the conflict, and viewed as accessories to the fact of perceived political hostilities against the populations and interests for which the group claims to speak. Whereas in old wars non-combatants and combatants *hors de combat* are not to be targeted because they do not, by their intentional actions, obstruct military operations to secure territory, in new wars they may be just as implicated in the supposed injustice the war is intended to rectify as are their soldiers in action.[21]

The upshot of this depiction is that Al Qaeda estimates that the citizens of the countries with whom it is at war bear a responsibility in the policies of their governments. This argument was stated straightforwardly in an interview granted by Osama Bin Laden to ABC journalist John Miller in May 1998:

> Any American who pays taxes to his government is our target because he is helping the American war machine against the Muslim nation ... Terrorizing oppressors and criminals and thieves and robbers is necessary for the safety of the people and for the protection of their property ... They have compromised our honour and our dignity and dare we utter a single word of protest, we are called terrorists. This is compounded injustice.

Such *democratisation of responsibility* and the licitness of the killing rest, it is argued, in the ability that citizens of the enemy countries have to elect and dismiss the representatives who take foreign policy decisions on their behalf. In the aforementioned ABC interview, Bin Laden added: 'We fight against their governments and all those who approve of the injustice they practice against us ... We fight them, and those who are part of their rule are judged in the same manner.' The argument was restated by Bin Laden in October 2002:

> By electing these leaders, the American people have given their consent to the incarceration of the Palestinian people, the demolition of Palestinian homes, and the slaughter of the children of Iraq. The American people have the ability and choice to refuse the policies of their government, yet time and again, polls show the American people support the policies of the elected government ... This is why the American people are not innocent. The American people are active members in all these crimes.

And again in April 2006:

> The war is a responsibility shared between the people and the governments. The war goes on and the people are renewing their allegiance to its rulers and masters. They send their sons to armies to fight us and they continue their financial and moral support while our countries are burned and our houses are bombed and our people are killed and no one cares for us.

Al Qaeda's strategy is one of liberalisation and expansion of the domain of conflict. Its *differentia specifica* is that it mutes and renders moot the Arab and Islamic governments, which are qualified theoretically to address these grievances, and it seeks to engage directly with the people of the states concerned, whom it renders coresponsible for their governments' actions. Further, the campaign is prosecuted sparingly as those Western countries that choose not to associate with the declared governmental enemies are spared. This notional decoupling is not, however, always necessarily evidenced as it contradicts the tactical indistinction upon which Al Qaeda's overarching military strategy rests.

This predicament highlights the problematic interoperability that Al Qaeda establishes between *ius ad bellum* (law governing recourse to force) and *ius in bello* (legally accepted behaviour in war). Paul Gilbert remarks astutely that the 'authority to fight involves two aspects. One is that those who fight should be under effective control so that the rules of war, in particular those designed for the protection of civilians, should be observed ... The second aspect of authority is that of being in a position to decide to go to war, that is to say, to determine whether one's purposes in doing so would be appropriate ones', adding that 'the problem with these conclusions is that they do not seem to touch the Islamic revolutionaries' own conception of what gives them authority to fight and what makes their intentions the right ones; and this raises questions, of course, about the applicability of just war theory across cultural boundaries'.[22]

Al Qaeda claims a valid *ius ad bellum* case. Dismissing, in the same vein, Arab and Muslim governments (and noting the security inefficacy of their structures of authority perceived to be assisting the enemy), it sets itself the task of deciding war as a proper authority – the legitimacy of which is anchored in significant claimed public support – whose just cause is a case of self-defence in the face of American 'aggression' (i.e., war as punishment of the oppression of Muslims). The group affirms a right intention of restoring peace in the region. Noting the nature of American operations, it claims to be acting in proportionate response and as a last resort.

What is novel, here, is the manner in which a private group has, in essence, turned Louis XIV's dictum 'l'État c'est moi' into a statement akin to 'la guerre c'est moi'. In so doing, Al Qaeda is taking the international system to pre-Westphalian, Hobbesian notions of legitimacy in the conduct of warfare.

> The Clausewitzian insistence that war is a rational instrument for the pursuit of state interest – 'the continuation of politics by other means' – constituted a secularisation of legitimacy that paralleled developments in other spheres of activity. Once state interest had become the dominant legitimation of war, then claims of just cause by non-state actors could no longer be pursued through violent means.[23]

In calling an end to that monopoly, Al Qaeda establishes its own claim to conduct war legitimately. Note that the consent of the population represented is understood as tacit; the unstated and unstatable conviction of many Muslims is that 'what goes around comes around'.

The third manner in which Al Qaeda manifests transformed war is the question of the identity of the actors. The characters now partaking of new conflicts have mutated, rendering identification more difficult. For Jean-Jacques Rousseau, war occurred – 240 years ago – not between man and man, but between states. The individuals who became involved in it were, argued the Swiss philosopher, enemies only by accident.[24] Contrapuntally, the leading conflict of our time takes the form of war between a major state and a group of a few thousand individuals. To be certain, the latter spring from states, which they in turn, for the most, have fought and sought to reform violently. Yet force is their *ultima ratio*, and legitimate force proceeds from a perceived right of self-defence which is substituted for statist, legal and decisive authority. Lacking a measurement matrix of this collapse of categories, the antiquated structures of international law fail to grasp such an evolution from 'impersonal' to 'personal' war.

THE LIMITS OF THE LAW

Al Qaeda's war has revealed important limitations in the manner
in which international law regulates warfare. This conflict has
simultaneously cast shafts of light on gaps in international
humanitarian law, in particular, and epitomised a return to
stripped-down concepts of opposition. The spectre of desuetude
hovers over the law of war. As one analyst remarks,

> war exists when a political entity attempts to compel an enemy by
> force – irrespective of whether this force complies with regulatory laws
> created by man or meets a specific juridical definition. Man's law is an
> artificial construct. It is not an immutable law, such as the law of physics,
> and hence a man's law may be (and often is) ignored or broken. The
> principles of warfare, on the other hand, apply whether man recognises
> them or not. They apply whenever war exists and, therefore, are not
> considered normative.[25]

That being as it may, international law can only function if
it is grounded in an expression and an assumption of equality
of the parties involved. The law of war is an exception to this
axiom. Whereas opponents agree to the rules because they
come to regard each other as equals, and desire an equality of
treatment in the expression of *ius belli*, such equality is rejected
forcefully today when it comes to transnational armed groups.
It is rejected, first and foremost, by the groups themselves who
shun awareness of and compliance with the law, but also by
states which, by virtue of their 'high contracting parties' status,
define the terms of the law.

Yet recognition of norms by actors involved in conflict
(domestic or international) is what makes standards relevant.
Law, in and of itself, is never complete nor all-encompassing.
Neither, as a dynamic aspect of human experience, is law
static. It is the combined construct and practice of law that
make it stand as a platform for rights and obligations. Legal
reasoning, interpretation and argumentation are meant to
allow for a systematic and systemic approach to the promotion
and defence of rights (to kill) and duties (to distinguish). That

approach leads, in turn, to the predictable implementation of law, not merely its theory.

This dimension of the primacy of the law – its 'rule', in effect – stands at the heart of the legal framework. It implies that all actors must appreciate (and respect) the added value of the legal approach, namely the insurance of protection associated with a system, which, though it may be imperfect, inconvenient and sometimes misguided, seeks to help regulate and advance a process.

In that respect, legal predictability is necessary for the state as it strengthens its robustness, but is not necessarily so for subnational armed groups which fancy non-linearity. Predictability is linear; it is grounded in the legality of the state, its administrative allocation of cost, vigorous prosecuting and delineated statehood – none of which is much relevant to stateless actors whose dividends are earned under asymmetry.

To be certain too, law is but a means to an end. It can be counterproductive, unfair and indeed inhuman (as in the case of law-sanctioned slavery of old). Moreover, definition of the law is an exclusionary process, and its implementation can be arbitrary. This cannot, however, mean that the relevance of the law or its imperfect-yet-necessary aspects are questioned. Rather, any law, including the one organising conflict, is the expression of a particular order, which in turn represents a power configuration. That order and that force are inseparable from their context. As such, they need constant examination, particularly since disconnects can develop between the values and interests protected by the law and the parties that are supposed to benefit from that system.

Finally, the strength of international humanitarian law lies in its unvariedness. Yet, today, that very predictability is being eroded because the referential point organising it, namely interstate symmetrical war, is vanishing. As the formal codification of the state's monopoly over the legitimate use of violence, international law is tautologously state-centred, state-defined and state-controlled; twenty-first century warfare is not. As we have seen, current war is democratised, open-ended and enlarged. Amid the proliferation of non-trinitarian patterns of war (across and beyond the state, the army and the citizens) and shifts in the position of civilians, the ritualisation and regulation of war have become problematic.

The existing procedure no longer generates a meaningful account of the new substance. Indeed, 'while international law grows in significance through trade organisations and human rights tribunals, it will play less of a role in the conduct of war because war will increasingly be unconventional and undeclared, and fought within states rather than between them'.[26] Nevertheless, scant attention is paid to these dimensions, and discussion of Al Qaeda's war continues to be marred by doctrinal insistence on its illegality. This, too, may no longer be tenable in light of contradictions in the scholarship and practice underscoring this view.

A social act, war is, first and foremost, organised violence between political units. For all its novelty, far from being an aberration or an anomaly, Al Qaeda's war is the outcome of a natural development whereby the perceived failure of particular states to act on behalf of populations and their interests has led to the creation of a regional entity seeking to undertake those martial responsibilities globally.

Cast in such light, Al Qaeda's is a claim to circumvent statehood, and particularly its monopoly over legitimate violence. At once inertial and curative, this disposition represents the epicentre of the organisation's ethos – one that cannot be reconciled readily with international law. Yet confutations abound:

> Is it armed action by sub-state actors per se that is objected to as somehow a threat to human rights? Surely not, for sometimes such action is undertaken to defend them. Is it specifically sub-state action across international boundaries? This too is sometimes claimed to be defensive and not without reason. Is it sub-state action that destabilises the borders within which law and order can be maintained? Again not, as there is a wider tolerance, on broadly liberal principles, of self-determinative struggles which have this effect than might otherwise seem desirable.[27]

In sum, while international law is depreciated, international military affairs are moving from a predictable framework of monopoly, distinction, concentration, brevity and linearity, wherein the role of the state has been attenuated, to an unpredictable order of privatisation, indifferentiation, dispersion, open-endedness and non-linearity, in which the place of non-state actors has become central.

Recognition of the paradigm modification unfolding before us has, hence, become imperative. A paradigm is composed of a set of assumptions that form a persistent representation of an order. Failure of the representations associated with these assumptions leads normally to its reconsideration. Paradigms of law and war inform the changing understanding of mutating international affairs regimes where neither full continuity nor complete change are obtained. In the case at hand, the correlation of forces, the nature of the wills clashing, and the adherence, and lack thereof, to particular normative values underscoring the existing configuration of the international legal and power order call for reorganised propositions to depict objectively, understand neutrally and regulate realistically such *bellum novae*.

Lest the disconnect between conceptual continuity and practical discontinuity persist, the danger of irrelevance of international law is for it to perpetuate a declamatory dynamic. International rules of war obviously cannot sustain that which has no safe and solid foundation in the social organisation of military affairs.[28] Yet a discernible complex reality – the war between sovereign, territorial, concrete US government and fragmented, global, abstract Al Qaeda – currently escapes codification.

A NEW TYPE OF ACTOR

The key prerequisite shift for a paradigm change is the introduction of actors or phenomena triggering ostensible alteration in the fundamental dynamics of a given system. Stateless, globalised, deterritorialised and untraceable, Al Qaeda is one such actor and its actions affect the existing international affairs regime in three main respects.

First, the geographical indeterminacy of the group's action speaks of the dissolution of territorial power. As the spatial dimension has been changed and militarised, the theatre of conflict has become global and points of interaction multiple. Al Qaeda operates in a fragmented geopolitical landscape wherein 'instead of being exported from the centre to the periphery, [jihad] will be imported from the periphery to the centre. And this immediately puts the idea of a centre itself in doubt by robbing it of one of its most important attributes – the ability to expand'.[29] Specifically, territory is problematic because it constitutes fixed property that needs to be protected permanently. Al Qaeda's dispersion engenders tactical superiority, which serves to equalise the organisation's strategic inferiority.

In the event, a battle*space* is replacing the battle*field*. To be certain, the latter was a nonvirtualisable invention following the modern codification of war. More importantly, the territorial principle was imposed originally as the instrument of the authority of governments. The very process of territory construction was linked, in effect, to the establishment of sovereignty, and was not determined by the abstract existence of a given identity.[30] With the breaking down of the rules of organised war, the expansion of the terrain – rendered easier by the transnational nature of the conflict between Al Qaeda and the United States and the reach of the parties (one's might, the other's agility) – is expressing a natural shift to a different cosmogony; one with manifest transgressions of the territorial paradigm: pluridimensionality, fluidity and complexity.

Second, the strategy devised and adopted by Al Qaeda marks the escalation of militarisation on the part of a non-state actor beyond traditional forms of terrorism with a redirecting of its effort to the centre of the political sphere. Categorically speaking, 'war is an act of lethal force between organized political entities for the purpose of achieving political goals by compelling an enemy to modify or surrender his own political objectives through weakening or destroying his will to resist'.[31]

Be that as it may, Al Qaeda's *modus operandi* is redefining international combat methods. As Münkler notes:

> Whereas guerrilla warfare is basically a defensive form of asymmetrisation, designed for use against a militarily superior occupying power, terrorism is the offensive form of the strategic asymmetrisation of force ... The offensive capacities of terrorists rest upon their logistical use of the civilian infrastructure of the country under attack, and at the same time on their conversion of it into a weapon.[32]

This form of conducting war has an important twofold implication for enduring principles of international humanitarian law, namely the obliteration of the combatant/civilian status categories and the refusal to distinguish between civilian and military targets. The strategy underscores specifically kamikaze attacks as a feature of modern conflicts that claim to be about retribution and restoring justice. In that respect, the canonical stigmatisation of suicide attacks stifles debate. As Mahmood Mamdani notes, 'we need to recognize the suicide bomber, first and foremost, as a category of soldier'.[33] A young Palestinian explains: 'I know I cannot stand in front of a tank that would wipe me out within seconds, so I use myself as a weapon. They call it terrorism. I say it is self-defence'.[34]

Table 2.3 Al Qaeda's Non-linear War

Motive	Punitive retaliation to aggressive policies
Rationale	Principle 1 *Substitution*
	Bypassing the state's monopoly of legitimate violence
	Principle 2 *Indiscrimination*
	Privatised collective responsibility
Strategy	Instrumentalisation of technological imbalance
	Disparity of forces as opportunity rather than constraint
Tactics	• Mobilisation of combatants across boundaries
	• Cell structure and spin-off groups
	• Use of high-profile civilian assets (planes, trains, ships, buses, hotels)

Third, the will and power to act militarily is claimed legitimately by a private entity. In other words, in the face of perceived oppression, a rational disputation arises whereby the authority to fight is no longer related solely to the state-centred authority that governs lawfully.

The impetus for such *captation de fonction* is twofold. It comes, on the one hand, from an evolutionary continuity beyond the values of the group (war's objective mutation), and, on the other hand, from a force-extender subjective principle of sense of deprivation (the group's political organising principles about restoring justice). Among the logical concomitants to such an approach pregnant with tactical possibilities is a conscious confusion of the two modes that speak to the manner war is conceived of, namely a maximisation of moral force.

In this respect, Al Qaeda is a sub-state, international armed group that is making a claim to a legitimate war against a group of countries regarded as oppressors. That pretension regards the use of indiscriminate force against civilians belonging to those countries, or those who publicly associate themselves with the authorities of these countries, as an acceptable method of warfare.

From the point of view of Al Qaeda, the policies enacted by the United States in the Middle East constitute therefore a *casus belli*. The group's reactive war is waged to redress an injury, but also to recover territorial property. The campaign is presented as a struggle against *dhulm* (injustice, offence) and therefore as mere retaliation in the face of provocations.

Bin Laden was explicit on this issue in his 1998 interview with ABC:

It is not enough for their people to show pain when they see our children being killed in Israeli raids launched by American planes, nor does this serve the purpose. What they ought to do is change their governments which attack our countries. The hostility that America continues to express against the Muslim people has given rise to feelings of animosity on the part of Muslims against America and against the West in general. Those feelings of animosity have produced a change in the behaviour of some crushed and subdued groups who, instead of fighting the Americans inside the Muslim countries, went on to fight them inside the United States of America itself.

Ayman al Dhawahiri was similarly explicit on this assignation of responsibility in a book he wrote in the autumn of 2001:

> It also transpires that in playing this role, the Western countries were backed by their peoples, who were free in their decision. It is true that they may be largely influenced by the media decision and distortion, but in the end they cast their votes in the elections to choose the governments that they want, pay taxes to fund their policy, and hold them accountable about how this money was spent. Regardless of method by which these governments obtain the votes of the people, voters in the Western countries ultimately cast their votes willingly.

If, arguably, the visiting of retribution is potentially tenable from an *ius ad bellum* point of view, the *ius in bello* dimension is more problematic – including from a religious point of view as suicide bombings also challenge two fundamental principles of Islamic ethics, namely the prohibition against suicide and the deliberate killing of non-combatants, which are also featured explicitly in the Koran and the prophet Mohammad's practice. The Koran intimates: 'And fight in God's cause against those who wage war against you, but do not transgress limits' (2:190). The prophet's tradition was summed up in a series of commands that he issued to his military forces going into battle, and which were perpetuated by the different caliphs:

Do not act treacherously,
Do not act disloyally,
Do not act neglectfully,
Do not mutilate,
Do not kill little children or old men,
Do not cut down trees,
Do not slaughter a sheep or a cow or a camel, except for food,
You will pass by people who devoted their lives in cloisters; leave them and their devotions alone.[35]

Put simply, the responsibilisation and resulting targeting of civilians cannot be reconciled with the central international humanitarian law tenet of distinction; the *ius in bello* principle of non-combatant immunity. Yet the cogency of Al Qaeda's novel claim rests on an indiscriminateness that is merely apparent. Holding the citizens of the state responsible individually and documenting the founding rationale for such conduct indicates effective control and a potential measure of respect for the rules. As it is, Al Qaeda has attacked both military (Pentagon, USS *Cole*) and civilian (World Trade Center, Atocha train station and London underground system) targets.

In a 20 October 2001 interview with the Kabul correspondent of Al Jazeera, which was not released by the network (but subsequently aired partly by CNN on 31 January 2002), Osama Bin Laden addressed the issue of targeting civilians at length:

The killing of innocent civilians, as America and some intellectuals claim, is really strange talk. Who said that our children and civilians are not innocent and that shedding their blood is justified? When we kill their innocents, the entire world from East to West screams at us ... Who said that our blood is not blood, but theirs is? ... Human nature makes people stand with the powerful without noticing it. When they talk about us, they know we will not respond to them ... So we kill their innocents, this is valid both religiously and logically. Some of the people who talk about this issue discuss it from a religious point of view. They say that the killing of innocents is wrong and invalid, and for proof, they say that the Prophet forbade the killing of women and children, and this is true. It is valid and has been laid down by the Prophet in an authentic tradition. However, this prohibition of the killing of children and innocents is not absolute. There are other texts that restrict it ... God's saying: 'And if you punish your enemy, O you believers in the Oneness of God, then punish them with the like of that with which you were afflicted' [Koran 16:126] ... The men that God helped [attack, on 11 September] did not intend to kill babies; they intended to destroy the strongest military power in the world, to attack the Pentagon that houses more than sixty-four thousand employees, a military centre that houses the strength and the military intelligence. The [twin] towers [were] an economic power and not a children's school or a residence. The general consensus is that those that were there were men that supported the biggest economic power in the world. They have to review their books. We treat others like they treat us. If they kill our women and our innocent people, we will kill their women and their innocent people until they stop doing so.[36]

Coming to grips with such metamorphosis of offence – and the strident leverage that Al Qaeda commands – means understanding the logic in which terrorism is used as a method of warfare, according to a principle of *in*discrimination whose rationale is negation of the notion of innocence of the civilian population, and imputation of collective responsibility to those who support the unjust actions of their government. Be that as it may, 'if terrorism *is* to be treated as a method of war, in accordance with the unjust war model, then there must be *some* legitimate targets which the terrorists could attack in consistence with the rules of war'.[37]

To be certain, there are self-imposed limitations to Al Qaeda's actions (no weapons of mass destruction have been used so far), but the civilian/military distinction is rejected formally by the group. Permissible warfare is channelled within aggrandisement of the principle of necessity (Arab states' failure to protect their citizens), literalisation of civilian responsibility (electoral support of aggressive policies), and acknowledgment of technological imbalance (instrumentalisation of asymmetry through modification of the *locus* and *tempo* of operations). It is argued that an extreme situation (of collapse of the power structures or fragmentation of power in the Muslim world) calls for extreme measures. In Clausewitzian fashion, war aims are pursued nakedly and no state patronage is needed. In many ways, this is the result of the deficiencies of the contemporary Arab state system and the concomitant rise of Islamist groups as a political and military force.

3

Purpose and Pattern

Human history is made by human beings. Since the struggle for control over territory is part of that history, so too is the struggle over historical and social meaning. The task for the critical scholar is not to separate one struggle from another, but to connect them, despite the contrast between the overpowering materiality of the former and the apparent otherworldly refinements of the latter.

Edward Said, *Orientalism*, 1978

Eliciting more disagreement than assent, the challenge represented by the newness of Al Qaeda is reinforced by existing analytical shortcomings. Al Qaeda's nature continues to baffle analysts and the language used to 'explain' it elides important distinctions. When its existence is not refuted, the group has been described, pell-mell, as a formula system, a venture capitalist firm, a commissioning editor, a newspaper, a television production, a publishing house, a wealthy university, a financial godfather, a transnational corporation, a franchise outfit and a multinational holding company. Such multiplicity of analogies betrays, first and foremost, the organisation's novelty.

Al Qaeda is a political movement with a demonstrated military ability, which has sought to bypass the state while co-opting its attributes and channelling its resources. Some analysts have posited that Al Qaeda is goal-oriented not rule-oriented, and that this sets it apart from state-sponsored groups. Within a fluid and dynamic approach, Al Qaeda has in fact concluded that given the current configuration of Arab politics, it is not possible to expect realistically the region's long-time a-dying regimes to defend the populations' interests.

The group then organised to achieve those goals and, in the process, effect a more legitimate social, political, economic and religious rule.

As the acme of a new generation of non-state actors, Al Qaeda has come to represent an organisation whose rough etiquette is violent action. However, the formulation of that use of force (in fact a military strategy) has been enacted in purely instrumentalist terms, and, in time, taken on an emphasised political mode. Between the late 1980s and the mid-2000s, the group went through four different phases, mutating in the course into a fully-fledged international political force.

1989–95: BIRTH AND STRATEGY DEVELOPMENT

Al Qaeda was born as a result of the failure of discredited Arab governments to defend their countries. The evolution towards armed politics of a group of Arab Islamists from the Middle East and North Africa allied with Asian Muslims was the consequence of a dual realisation, wherein private actors came to the conclusion that their states were too weak to defend their citizenry, but equally too strong to be overtaken. At the core of the group's genesis stands, thus, a mixture of pragmatism and defiance, not, as is often argued, hopelessness and despair.

The ascendancy of this rationale meant that domestic failure and repression of the 'near enemy' (*al adou al qareeb*) should be separated tactically from the fight against the 'far enemy' (*al adou al ba'eed*), namely that party which allows the situation to persist and benefits from it. The notion of focus on the latter led inevitably to taking the battle to the United States' territory. (A portent of this strategy was the operation conducted by Hizballah in Beirut on 18 April 1983 against the US Marine barracks and the French paratroopers' headquarters, which killed 241 Marines and 58 paratroopers and led to the United States' withdrawal from Lebanon.)

The strategy meant too the husbanding of financial and logistical resources and the formation of professional, disciplined and dependable soldiers, as well as a corps of officers and permanent contacts. A Palestinian named Abdallah Azzam, who had emerged as leader of those Arabs who travelled to Afghanistan in the 1980s to help the Afghans resist the Soviet invasion, set up an office of logistical coordination for the affairs of the 'Arab Afghans', the *Maktab al Khadamat lil Mujahideen al Arab* (also know as *Maktab al Dhiyafa* or hospitality house).[1] This way station, which functioned as an international bureau and serviced some 25,000 individuals, served as the matrix for what, in time, would become Al Qaeda.

The broad outlines of an organisation that would outlast the Afghanistan conflict emerged in earnest in late 1987 with the winding down of the Soviet campaign in the country. Before his death in November 1989, the Jenin-born, Al-Azhar-trained, Islamabad University lecturer Azzam had put in place the elements of such an international army in partnership with Osama Bin Laden, who initially left Saudi Arabia for Pakistan in December 1979 and set up his own support station for the Arab mujahideen in Afghanistan, the *Beit al Ansar* (House of the Followers). Ayman al Dhawahiri, who migrated to Afghanistan from Egypt in 1985, later joined Bin Laden in spearheading these efforts. The concept of an all-Arab/Muslim legion to wage warfare against the United States was fleshed out eventually in late 1989 at a meeting in Khost, Afghanistan. The entity was originally dubbed *Al Qaeda al Askariya* (the military base).[2]

International recruits, including some coming from the United States, were trained in Afghanistan as early as 1985. The transformation that occurred from then on meant that the new army would not be operating solely or primarily in territorial contiguity (e.g., Afghanistan or Egypt), and that, in departing from 1970s- and 1980s-type terrorism, it would shift from loosely coordinated quantitative attacks to carefully planned quality operations.

That the ambition of the new Qaeda actor was indeed to displace the state's military function – which it regarded as both illegitimate and dangerously defective – is underscored by the unsuccessful offer made by Osama Bin Laden to the Saudi government in 1991 to use his organisation to expel the Iraqi forces that had invaded Kuwait in August of that year. Subsequently, in April 1994, the Saudi royal family stripped Bin Laden of his passport and his citizenship.[3] Bin Laden then moved the organisation to Sudan, where he headquartered his operations and spent in excess of 300 million US dollars mostly in road works and construction projects. All in all, Al Qaeda was, at varying degrees and in different capacities, present in the Sudan from December 1991 to May 1996. Bin Laden's interest in Sudanese affairs remained, as attested by his call to Muslims, in April 2006, to resist Western intervention in the Darfur region.

Besides establishing the parameters of a global strategy, this initial phase also allowed Al Qaeda to effect discipline, training and unit cohesion within its ranks. The organisation initially followed a hierarchical system where a leader (Osama Bin Laden, known as 'Abu Abdallah' to his troops) and a deputy (Ayman al Dhawahiri, often referred to as 'the doctor') received the advice of a 31 member consultative council (*Majliss al Shura*) divided into five operational committees: military, religious affairs, financial matters, media and publicity, and logistics.

Headed by Abu Obaida al Banshiri and Mohammad Atef (killed respectively in May 1996 and November 2001), the military committee oversaw activities of local units (notably, the 300-strong battle-tested 055 Brigade, which was integrated into the Taliban-run Army of the Islamic Emirate of Afghanistan to fight the Northern Alliance) and their training in a number of camps in Kabul, Khost, Mahavia, Jalalabad, Kunar, Kandahar, Tora Bora and Liza, several of which were built using equipment previously owned by Bin Laden's construction company. That committee was also in charge of the development and supervision of a growing number of international cells in Europe (Germany, Italy, Britain), South-East Asia (Singapore, Malaysia, the Philippines), and East Africa (Tanzania, Kenya).

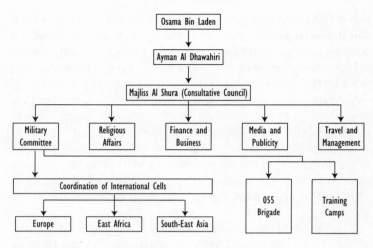

Figure 3.1   Al Qaeda in the 1990s

1996–2001: WAR PLANS

Having put in place the components of a far-flung force, the leadership of Al Qaeda focused its attention on the elaboration of a war strategy that would take the form of a sustained campaign on different centres of gravity, with a view to spreading the enemy's attention and exposing it. To be certain, consideration of operational matters continued. Hence, a training manual meant to serve as a reference for the soldiers, the *Encyclopaedia of the Jihad*, was released in Afghanistan in 1996 and transferred to CD-ROM in 1999; it covered different aspects of guerrilla warfare, use of explosives, surveillance protocol, kamikaze attacks and interrogation techniques.

This phase of the history of Al Qaeda was concerned with maintaining training camps, assembling a coalition of operatives and overseeing the preparation of several parallel missions. In May 1996, Osama Bin Laden and his close companions relocated from the Sudan to Afghanistan, where the Taliban led by Mullah Mohammad Omar had recently taken control of most of the country. Having considered other locations (the Yemen, notably), a choice was made to settle in Afghanistan and wage battle not in that country, which was regarded as a sanctuary, but on US-related international targets in a variety of geographical sectors. In that sense, the alliance that took place between Al Qaeda and the Taliban was merely tactical, and based not on religious grounds (the latter follows an extremist form of Islam alien to the vast majority of Arabs and Muslims, Al Qaeda's Islam is militant and Salafi but its conservatism is relatively familiar to large numbers) but on the fact that the Taliban actually controlled a state.

Reversing the state-sponsoring rule, Bin Laden would then engage in subsidising a state (whereas in the Sudan and in Saudi Arabia he had attempted merely to influence state practice) and consolidating the links with the Taliban. Some 2,000 battle-hardened Qaeda soldiers (the 055 Brigade) were integrated into the Taliban forces. Such geopolitical latitude illustrated appositely a desire to shift from a local-defensive to an international-offensive approach.

In addition to the amount of attacks, Al Qaeda leaders would also concentrate on developing a new type of operations against their enemies in the West. As Bin Laden explained in a 24 November 1996 interview with the editor-in-chief of the London-based Arabic daily newspaper, *Al Qods al Arabi*, Abdel Bari Atwan:[4]

> Preparations for major operations take a certain amount of time, unlike minor operations. If we wanted small actions, the matter would have been carried out easily ... The nature of the battle calls for operations of a specific type that will make an impact on the enemy and this calls for excellent preparations.

In the Declaration of War against the United States made by Al Qaeda four months earlier, such strategy, rooted in a tactical acknowledgment of the military imparity, was noted similarly:

> Due to the *imbalance of power* between our armed forces and the enemy forces, a suitable means of fighting must be adopted, namely

using *fast-moving light* forces that work under complete secrecy ... It is wise in the present circumstances for the armed military forces not to be engaged in *conventional fighting* with the forces of the ... enemy ... unless a big advantage is likely to be achieved; and the great losses induced on the enemy side that would shake and destroy its foundations and infrastructure ... spread rumours, fear, and discouragement among the members of the enemy forces. (Emphasis added.)

Planning operations properly and moving on the time continuum is a defining feature of the organisation's strategy. In his January 2006 message to the American people, Bin Laden explained thus the absence of attacks in the United States since September 2001: 'As for the delay in carrying out similar operations in America, this was not due to failure to breach your security measures. Operations are under preparation, and you will see them on your own ground once they are finished'.

The focus of the energy, during the 1990s, was both on setting a sophisticated infrastructure and identifying and recruiting highly motivated individuals who would be subsequently short-listed for operations to enact an unprecedented battle plan: major attacks in the United States. In a videotaped will made in the spring of 2001 and aired on Al Jazeera on 17 April 2002, Ahmed al Haznawi, one of the 19 hijackers of the 11 September 2001 operation, declared: 'Today we are killing them in the midst of their homes. It is time to kill Americans in their heartland'.

Such transformation did not completely escape analysts. Following the 25 June 1996 attack on the Al Khobar Towers apartment complex housing US Air Force personnel in Dhahran, Saudi Arabia, the head of the United States Central Command declared at a Senate Armed Services Committee hearing: 'Recently, we have seen growth in "transnational" groups, comprised of fanatical Islamic extremists, many of whom fought in Afghanistan and now drift to other countries with the aim of establishing anti-Western fundamentalist regimes by destabilizing traditional governments and attacking US and Western targets'.[5] Such recognition notwithstanding, the 9/11 Commission reported that 'until 1996, hardly anyone in the US government understood that Osama Bin Laden was an inspirer and organizer of the new terrorism [...] While we know now that Al Qaeda was formed in 1988, at the end of the Soviet occupation of Afghanistan, the intelligence community did not describe this organization, at least in documents we have seen, until 1999'.[6]

As Al Qaeda was assembling its war apparatus, its leaders started making public a *sui generis* international case for war against the United States. Thus, in 1997–98, Osama Bin Laden granted a number of interviews with international media outlets and held a press conference. The opening salvo of that communication strategy took place in April 1997 when Bin Laden granted an interview to CNN journalist Peter Bergen (aired on May 12). In it, Bin Laden declared:

> We believe the United States is responsible directly for those who were killed in Palestine, Lebanon, and Iraq. This American government abandoned humanitarian feelings by these hideous crimes. It transgressed all bounds and behaved in a way not witnessed before by any power or any imperialist power in the world. The United States today has set a double standard, calling whoever goes against its injustice a terrorist. It wants to occupy our countries, steal our resources, impose on us agents to rule us ... and wants us to agree to all this. If we refuse to do so, it will say, 'You are terrorists'.[7]

In time, war was declared on America. Twice. On 23 August 1996, Bin Laden and supporters issued a Declaration of War against the Americans Occupying the Land of the Two Holy Places. On 23 February 1998, Bin Laden issued a second declaration of war stating that to 'kill Americans and their allies – civilian and military – is an individual duty for every Muslim who can do it in any country in which it is possible to do so, in order to liberate the Al Aqsa mosque and the Holy Mosque, and in order for their armies to move out of the lands of Islam, defeated and unable to threaten any Muslim'. That statement was forwarded to the London-based newspaper *Al Qods al Arabi* by Qaeda military committee leader Mohammad

Atef for publication, and it was followed by a press conference in May 1998. During that phase, Bin Laden also maintained an office in London headed by Khaled al Fawaz.

These pronouncements followed an extraordinarily insistent logic in which US policies in the Middle East were regarded as constitutive of a *casus belli*. Initial engagements – notably the attack on the Office of Program Management of the US-trained Saudi National Guard in Riyadh on 13 November 1995 and the August 1996 Dhahran bombing – were followed by more frontal attacks. On 7 August 1998, Al Qaeda conducted two simultaneous bombings of the United States embassies in Nairobi, Kenya and Dar es Salaam, Tanzania. On 11 August, an Islamic Liberation Army of the People of Kenya, in all likelihood a junior off-shoot of Al Qaeda, issued a statement (from London) whose rationale and language for the attacks was consistent with the 1996 and 1998 war declarations. It noted: 'The Americans humiliate our people, they have occupied the Arabian Peninsula, they extract our riches, they enforce a blockade, and they support Israel, our archenemy who occupies the Al Aqsa mosque'.

The United States responded with Operation Infinite Reach on 20 August firing cruise missiles on training camps in Khost, Afghanistan and a pharmaceutical plant in Khartoum – two locations associated with Al Qaeda. The battle was joined. Again, this realisation was not lost on the American side. In a 4 December 1998 internal memorandum on Al Qaeda, CIA Director George Tenet wrote: 'We are at war'.[8]

The sophistication of Al Qaeda's military operations continued to grow throughout 1990s. A thwarted attempt to bomb an American warship off the Yemeni coast, the USS *The Sullivans*, on 3 January 2000, was followed by a successful kamikaze attack on another vessel, the USS *Cole*, the following 12 October. Infiltration operations were conducted similarly by Qaeda operatives. At least one individual, Ali Mohammad, joined Al Qaeda after accessing classified documents while serving in the US Army. Mohammad was a US Army sergeant assigned to a Special Forces unit at Fort Bragg, North Carolina.

In the early 1990s, he trained Al Qaeda recruits in surveillance techniques, cell structures and detailed reconnaissance.[9]

While research, preparation and training for a fourfold assault on New York and Washington were underway, the organisation's leadership accelerated the formation of its foot soldiers in Afghanistan. Though accurate information about the numbers of those trainees is not available, and public figures oscillate between 10,000 and 100,000, it can be estimated realistically that 10,000 to 20,000 individuals were trained in these camps. Of those, 5,000 to 10,000 may still be active and scattered around the world.

On 11 September 2001, an Al Qaeda commando, initially assembled in Germany and led by Egyptian architect Mohammad Atta, hijacked near-simultaneously four American domestic airliners. It crashed two into the World Trade Center in New York, and one into the Pentagon in Washington, DC. More than 3,000 Americans perished.

2002–3: REGROUPING AND PRIVATISING

Before the United States and the United Kingdom attacked Taliban forces in Afghanistan in October 2001 in retaliation for the New York and Washington operations, Al Qaeda's leadership had realised that a full engagement with American and British forces in Afghanistan would be tantamount to suicide. In the face of overwhelming power – though the United States had adopted a scaled-down approach to invasion, wherein local co-opted forces (the Northern Alliance, in particular) were enlisted and paid to fight on behalf of the United States – a strategic retreat was chosen. For Al Qaeda, the risk-minimising objective was to slow the Western forces' advance, as per Sun Tzu's maxim that 'one defends when his strength is inadequate', and Van Creveld's axiom that 'a belligerent who is weaker than the enemy cannot afford to be worn down'.[10]

In the event, between the autumn of 2001 and the spring of 2002, Al Qaeda's forces – which must be distinguished from Taliban contingents – were not depleted as much as they were reallocated. With the battles of Tora Bora (December 2001) and

Shahi Kowt (March 2002) lasting three weeks each, this elastic defence relying on mobile forces was paralleled by a scaling up of international operations and an investment in global tactical relationships.

Faced with the objective possibility of a copycat phenomenon and the subjective aim to maximise politically its 11 September military success, and no longer able to enjoy a centralised sanctuary, Al Qaeda's leadership encouraged the proliferation of mini-Al Qaedas, groups that would be connected loosely to a 'mother Al Qaeda' (*Al Qaeda al Oum*), but which would be independent and viable enough to act on their own within a regional context. Such shift from 'thinking locally and acting globally' to 'thinking globally and acting locally' relied on self-contained, mission-oriented strategic units in South-East Asia, Western Europe, East Africa, North Africa, Jordan and Iraq, the Gulf and, possibly, North America.

In order to maximise its political and military impact, Al Qaeda has distinguished itself by generally opting for simultaneous, multi-track operations, rather than single attacks. Al Qaeda al Oum is fully aware of the effect of this

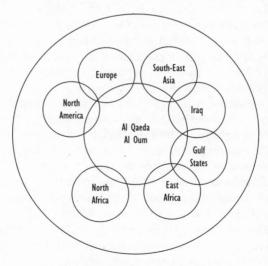

Figure 3.2   Al Qaeda in the 2000s

fissile strategy on its enemies. In his October 2004 message to the American people, Bin Laden remarked: 'All that we have to do is to send two mujahideen to the furthest point east to raise a piece of cloth on which is written Al Qaeda, in order to make the [US] generals race there to cause America to suffer human, economic and political losses without their achieving for it anything of note other than some benefits for their private companies'.

As an integrative force, the structure headed by Osama Bin Laden and Ayman al Dhawahiri provides an umbrella to two types of operations: those directly commissioned by Al Qaeda al Oum (in all likelihood from Pakistan or Afghanistan through a complex network of international contacts) and usually conducted in the Western metropolises (New York, Washington, Madrid, London) by educated, technology-savvy operators familiar with Western urban settings and those subcontracted, suggested or inspired to more populist, affiliated or associated groups in the periphery (Casablanca, Istanbul, Bali, Djerba). Hence, aside from the war in Iraq, between 2002 and 2006, the United States and seven of their Western allies (the United Kingdom, Spain, Italy, Australia, Israel, France and Germany) were the targets of 18 major attacks in 11 countries (Tunisia, Pakistan, Yemen, Indonesia, Kuwait, Spain, Saudi Arabia, the United Kingdom, Egypt, Kenya and Morocco) with a total of 775 people killed.

In an autumn 2001 book entitled *Knights Under the Prophet's Banner* – excerpts of which were published by the London-based, Arabic-language daily *Al Sharq al Awsat* on 2 December 2001 – Ayman al Dhawahiri had explained the approach and the cost-effective rationale of these measures, namely 'the need to inflict the maximum casualties against the opponent, for this is the language understood by the West, no matter how much time and effort such operations take ... The targets as well as the type and method of weapons used must be chosen to have an impact on the structure of the enemy and deter it enough to stop its brutality'. In Iraq, after 2003, this eventually took the form of ambushes, guerrilla tactics and small-scale engagements, as well as kidnappings, suicide bombings and beheadings.

In this same phase, Al Qaeda reserved, as well, the right to reciprocate should non-conventional weaponry be used by its enemies. On 10 November 2001, Osama Bin Laden declared in an interview in *Dawn* with Pakistani journalist Hamid Mir: 'If America uses chemical or nuclear weapons against us, then we may retort with chemical and nuclear weapons as a deterrent'. Subsequently, a Saudi scholar, Sheikh Nasser Ibn Hamid al Fahd, authored an *amicus curiae*-like treatise justifying the potential use of weapons of mass destruction by Al Qaeda, noting that civilian casualties are acceptable if they are the by-product of an attack intended to defeat massively the enemy.

Al Fahd argued: 'The situation in this regard is that if those engaged in jihad establish that the evil of the infidels can be repelled only by attacking them at night with weapons of mass destruction, they may be used even if they annihilate all the infidels'. He added:

Scholars have agreed that it is permissible to bombard an enemy with a catapult and similar things. As everyone knows, a catapult stone does not distinguish between women, children and others; it destroys anything that it hits, buildings or otherwise. This proves that the principle of destroying the infidels' lands and killing them if the Jihad requires it and those in authority over the Jihad decide so is legitimate.[11]

A characteristic of this phase is that, for the first time in its history, the organisation was on the defensive and suffering setbacks, chiefly the loss of Afghanistan as a base and the arrest or death of a few key figures, notably Mohammad Atef (Abu Hafs al Masri, head of the military committee, killed during a 14 November 2001 US air strike on Kabul), Zein al Abidin Mohammad Hussein (Abu Zubayda, director of external operations, captured in Faisalabad, Pakistan, on 28 March 2002), and Ramzi Ben al Shaiba and Khaled Sheikh Mohammad (respectively coordinator and planner of the 11 September 2001 operation, arrested on 11 September 2002 in Karachi and 1 March 2003 in Rawalpindi). Yet, for two reasons, these hardships did not affect the organisation's ability to function: displacement from the camps was anticipated, and the detained officers were replaced rapidly.

It is important to differentiate the functions that the central organ, Al Qaeda al Oum, and its peripheral branches, the regional cells, saw themselves as performing during this phase. The roles included, in particular, an unspoken differentiation of the type of enemies targeted. For instance, though they would later alter their thinking on the matter, Bin Laden and al Dhawahiri came to tolerate a level of violence on the part of the Iraqi Qaeda that was higher than the more discerning threshold they applied to operations elsewhere, particularly those attacks they commissioned in Western centres. In the Iraq case, this came, as well, to encompass a lack of pronouncement on Abu Masub al Zarqawi's beheadings of Western hostages and attacks on the Shi'a, something that Al Qaeda al Oum had not done. As one observer notes:

Al Qaeda leaders like Osama Bin Laden or Ayman al Dhawahiri have never been known to either preach or practice anti-Shi'a politics, indeed the opposite, with Bin Laden repeatedly urging Muslims to ignore internal differences and even appearing to uphold the Islamic credentials of Shiite Iran by comparing the longed-for ouster of the Saudi monarch to the expulsion of the Shah.[12]

Bin Laden had indeed urged his troops to refrain from sectarian strife, stating, in the 1996 Declaration of War, that 'there is a duty on the Muslims to ignore the minor differences amongst themselves'.

2004–6: WAR AND DIPLOMACY

Starting in 2004, Al Qaeda began reorienting its strategic and tactical direction. Between mid-2004 and mid-2006, Al Qaeda opened and closed a window for possibly ceasing its hostilities on the United States and its European allies. In the face of a lack of engagement with two offers of truce it extended, respectively, to Europe in April 2004 and the United States in January 2006 (both times, it left the offer 'on the table' for three months), it poised itself to return to transnational attacks on Western civilians, which it continued to regard as sharing the war responsibility of their governments.

At the same time, the organisation metastasised from a hierarchical to a decentralised, multicentric organisation. The relocation and repositioning of its forces went hand in hand with a new-found emphasis on its politico-diplomatic message. Ever borrowing attributes of the state, in 2004–6, Al Qaeda al Oum struck private and public alliances, offered truces, impacted on elections and, overall, gained international stature beyond a mere security threat. Moreover, an economic discourse was featured increasingly in its panoply, with multiple references, in Bin Laden and al Dhawahiri's regular messages, to the heavy cost of the war effort (particularly in Iraq and Afghanistan) to the US economy.

Al Qaeda al Oum has immersed itself in the political process of countries in Europe, the Middle East and the United States (as well as parts of Asia, particularly in Pakistan and Indonesia). On 11 March 2004, three days before Spain's legislative elections, in which the political party of Prime Minister José María Aznar, the Popular Party (PP), was forecasted the winner, a regional, North African-dominated cell of Al Qaeda in Europe (also known as 'the Brigades of Abu Hafs al Masri' after Mohammad Atef) detonated ten explosive devices aboard four commuter trains approaching the Atocha train station in Madrid, killing 191 individuals and injuring close to 2,000. Aznar's government, which had actively supported the United States' war effort in Iraq contributing troops, insisted on the responsibility of the Basque separatist group Euskadi ta Askatasuna (ETA). The following Sunday, the PP lost the elections to the Socialist Party led by José Luis Rodríguez Zapatero, who ordered the 1,300 Spanish soldiers out of Iraq on 18 April.

On 30 October 2004, four days before the American presidential elections, Osama Bin Laden sent a videotaped message to the American people 'concern[ing] the ideal way to prevent another Manhattan [attack], and deal[ing] with the war and its causes and consequences', in which he stated: 'Your security is not in the hands of [Democratic Party candidate John] Kerry, nor [President George W.] Bush, nor Al Qaeda. No. Your security is in your own hands. And every state that does not play with our security has automatically guaranteed its own security'. (The word used for 'state' (*wilaya*) had a purposeful double-entendre as it also refers to district area – in other words, Bin Laden was simultaneously warning the state of Ohio and the country as a whole.)

The following 27 December, Al Jazeera aired an audiotaped message in which Bin Laden advised the Iraqi people not to take part in the 30 January 2005 elections, explaining that the Constitution which the US Civil Administrator in Iraq, L. Paul Bremmer, had sponsored was illegitimate and divisive, and confirmed, 'for the record', that Jordanian Islamist militant Abu Musab al Zarqawi (Ahmad Fadl Nazzal al Khalayla) was the 'Emir' of Al Qaeda in Iraq, endorsing his struggle against the Americans, other occupation forces and Iraqi 'collaborators', and urging Iraqis to listen to him. On 17 October, al Zarqawi had published a statement on an Islamist website in which he claimed allegiance to Bin Laden, changing the name of his most recent organisation from *Al Tawhid wa al Jihad* (Unity and Holy War) to *Munadhamat al Qaeda fi Bilad al Rafidayn* (Organisation of Al Qaeda in Mesopotamia). Bin Laden welcomed that pledge deeming it 'an important step in unifying the fighters in establishing the state of righteousness and ending the state of injustice'. When, in 2006, reports of strains between al Zarqawi and Bin Laden circulated, a few weeks before his killing on 7 June, al Zarqawi released a videotaped message on 25 April in which he restated his full allegiance to Bin Laden.

In all likelihood, for a significant period of time, both soft and hard civilian and military targets will continue to be hit by Al Qaeda through the use of well-honed, low-cost, high-impact operations. A repeat of an attack such as the 11 September 2001 (United States), 11 March 2004 (Spain) or 7 July 2005 (United Kingdom) operations will in all likelihood be attempted, though it will take longer to prepare as infiltration in Western countries has become more difficult (thus factoring in Von Clausewitz's 'uncertainty' and 'friction' notions affecting the normal conduct of warfare). Like any army, Al Qaeda will persevere in seeking to expand its portfolio of operations until its goals are met. As Martin Van Creveld remarks, in war:

> an action that has succeeded once will likely fail when it is tried for the second time. It will fail, not *in spite* of having succeeded once but *because* its very success will probably put an intelligent opponent on its guard. The same reasoning also works in reverse. An operation having failed once, the opponent may conclude that it will not be repeated. Once he believes it will not be repeated, the best way to ensure success is precisely to repeat it.[13]

As Al Qaeda al Oum and its three official representations – Al Qaeda in Mesopotamia, Al Qaeda in Europe and Al Qaeda in the Gulf – as well as secret units and other associated militant Islamists continue their regional and international actions, we have witnessed, in the period 2002–6, a semi-public, internal debate on the acceptability and viability of attacks against civilians. If the principle of indiscrimination remains the mainstay of that discussion, interestingly there have been statements seeking to limit the perimeter of what can be targeted legitimately.

In 2004, Abu Mohammad al Maqdissi (Mohammad Taher al Burqawi), the original mentor of Abu Musab al Zarqawi – the two men had spent time in prison together in Jordan between 1994 and 1999 – wrote an open letter to the latter entitled 'Al Zarqawi: Support and Advice, Hopes and Fears'. In it, al Maqdissi argued: 'One should not target those that do not partake of combat, even if they are Infidels or Christians. Nor should one attack their churches or places of worship'. When the 27 victims of a 14 July 2005 suicide bombing carried out in Baghdad turned out to be children, al Zarqawi's Al Qaeda in Mesopotamia issued a statement the same day denying that it was responsible for that particular attack.[14]

Similarly, following the triple suicide bombing that killed 56 people, mostly Arab civilians, in the Grand Hyatt, Radisson SAS and Days Inn hotels in Amman on 9 November 2005, Al Qaeda in Mesopotamia issued two statements explaining the reasons for the attack, ostensibly with a view to justify them before Jordanians:

> We have struck only after becoming confident that [the hotels] are centres for launching war on Islam ... [These hotels were] favourite places for the work of intelligence organs, especially those of the Americans, the Israelis and some Western European countries ... Let everyone know that we will never hesitate in targeting these places wherever they are.[15]

Earlier, on 18 May, al Zarqawi had indicated that civilian collateral damage was acceptable in the pursuit of the war against the enemies of Muslims. He had declared:

> The shedding of Muslim blood ... is allowed in order to avoid the greater evil of disrupting Jihad. God knows that we were careful not to kill Muslims, and we have called off many operations in the past to avoid losses ... but we cannot kill infidels without killing some Muslims. It is unavoidable.[16]

To round out the picture of those developments, it is particularly crucial to take full stock of the intricate set of relationships within the ever-changing Al Qaeda. Starting in 2005, we witnessed a further emancipation of the regional cells; a *mise en abîme* of the very process that led to the rise of Al Qaeda al Oum itself. Hence, Al Qaeda in Mesopotamia began to conduct regional attacks beyond Iraq. As the original Al Qaeda had targeted Saudi Arabia and the United States, Al Qaeda in Mesopotamia has gone after Jordan and the United States (and allies) in Iraq. Al Zarqawi's first operations were the assassination of US diplomat Laurence Foley in Amman on 28 October 2002 and the bombing of the Jordanian embassy in Iraq on 7 August 2003. The Saudi/Jordanian dimensions are also informed significantly by Bin Laden's and al Zarqawi's respective nationalities and their desire to unseat the Sauds and the Hashemites. On 19 August, Al Qaeda in Mesopotamia fired rockets at a US Navy ship off the port of Aqaba. Indeed, it was Jordanian intelligence that was reportedly key in locating al Zarqawi and instrumental in enabling the US missile strike that killed him and several of his men on 7 June 2006.

Though minor, other similar regional developments using the same matrix took place in the larger Arab and Muslim world. Hence, the Algeria-based Salafist Group for Predication and Combat (GSPC), which had made allegiance to Al Qaeda al Oum in September 2003, threatened to attack France.

At times, it seemed that this acquisition of capacity on the part of the Iraqi cell, the violence that characterised al Zarqawi's methods, as well as the man's demonstrated potential for independence (in the late 1990s, he was heading his own training camps in Afghanistan separately from Bin Laden) were not necessarily wholly welcomed by the central organ. As Bin Laden seemed to pursue a strategy designed to render the largest possible number of Westerners aware of his political rationale for using force and enacting a diplomatic overture, and with al Dhawahiri echoing forcefully that reasoning (though with acerbic ideological commentary), the high media resonance of al Zarqawi's tactics, notably the beheadings of American hostages, was potentially endangering the cogency of that approach. What is more, possibilities of 'horizontal allegiance' developed with, for instance, the leader of the Saudi branch of Al Qaeda, Saleh al Oofi (killed in August 2005), pledging allegiance to al Zarqawi on 17 March 2004.

By mid-2006, however, Bin Laden seemed poised to forego the diplomatic track he had unilaterally opened in the spring of 2004. That his 23 April message of warning to the West was followed two days later by a videotaped message from al Zarqawi (who had previously been silent for three months), in turn followed three days later by a new message from al Dhawahiri, was a spectacular indication of Al Qaeda's ability to coordinate tactics transnationally, as well as a harbinger of renewed violence.

4

Fallacies and Primacies

The ideological cast of mind is necessarily hostile to genuine inquiry and critical thinking – to the testing of hypotheses, the search for and serious evaluation of counter-evidence, the revision or abandonment of key assumptions. For it is in the nature of ideology that the truth is considered to be already known.

Owen Harries, 'Suffer the Intellectuals', 2005

The history of Al Qaeda and its conflict with the United States and allies indicates that the events of 11 September 2001 were not gratuitous. The attack was a military operation, researched and planned since at least 1996, and conducted by a trained commando in the context of a war that had been declared officially and publicly in 1996 and again in 1998. The operation targeted two military objects (the Pentagon and the White House) and a civilian facility regarded as the symbol of the United States' economic and financial power (the World Trade Center).

The former head of the anti-Bin Laden unit at the Central Intelligence Agency notes:

The September 11 attacks were not apocalyptic onslaughts on Western civilization. They were country-specific attacks meant to inflict substantial, visible, and quantifiable human and economic destruction on America. The attacks were also meant to inflict psychological damage on Americans. The attacks were acts of war and had limited goals, which were achieved; intellectual honesty forbids describing them as efforts to destroy such unquantifiable things as our freedom or a way of life.[1]

The assault was the culmination of a larger campaign, which forecasted impact and planned for the enemy's reaction. The attack was, more importantly, a military act designed to surprise and gain the tactical and psychological upper hand; aims that were achieved. As Karl Von Clausewitz noted, 'a great destructive act inevitably exerts on all other actions, and it is exactly at such times that the moral factor is, so to speak, the most fluid element of all, and therefore spreads most easily to affect everything else'.[2]

However, such novelty and quickening of momentum have not been matched by the necessary programme of inquiry. The reductionism that characterises understanding of the mechanics of Al Qaeda (i.e., its depiction as nothing but a powerful terrorist group) partakes of a larger, more problematic, pattern of misrepresentation of the nature of the organisation's *modus essendi*. Al Qaeda's motives have been misrepresented, dismissed or ridiculed. In the face of operations such as the 11 September attacks and the geopolitical magnitude of their aftermath with the wars in Afghanistan and Iraq, speculation and jejune animosity are not appropriate modes of explanation and policy responses to lethal war.

MISLEADING EXPLANATIONS

Paradoxically, Al Qaeda's war on the United States remains documented inadequately and presented often as resistant to explanation (e.g., 'What does Al Qaeda want?'). In that context, and a mental horizon dominated by the accretion of emotional commentary and ideological amplification, the re-emergence of a crusading spirit is not to be taken too lightly. As was the case in previous epochs, after September 2001, 'the greatest minds of the ... Western world – the most profound, distinguished, subtle ..., illuminated ... thinkers ..., all bent their heads and their knees before the spirit of the crusade. They all subscribed – rarely with silence, often with admirable eloquence – to the declaration that it was necessary to eliminate those who had been ... declared enemies'.[3] Michael Ignatieff, for instance, argued that 'the norms that govern a war on terror are not the monopoly of government ... [S]tandards for a war on terror will be set by adversarial moral competition'.[4]

Overwhelmingly martial, most scholarship on Al Qaeda can be divided into three rough categories, namely the group's irrationality, fundamentalism and hatred. Other leading explanations of the animus of Al Qaeda emphasise poverty (as a source of terrorism), criminality (as a way to profit), and barbarism (to satiate bestial goals). On the first aspect, the social profile of both the senior leadership of the organisation (a millionaire, a surgeon of the old Cairote bourgeoisie) and the mid-level operators (PhDs such as Mohammad Atta, polyglots like Ziad Jarrah) and recent research indicate that the group's motivations are not to be found in economic deprivation. Similarly, and in spite of explicit statements to that effect by United States and United Kingdom officials (in particular the October 2001 British dossier), no allegations of criminal activity by Al Qaeda, regarding for instance drug trafficking in Afghanistan, have been substantiated to this day. Finally, and in spite of an increased level of violence since the 2003 war in Iraq, the consistent presence of political demands as part of the organisation's *casus belli* show that violence per se is not what motivates Al Qaeda.[5]

Yet an admixture of these conceptions – which achieved normative supremacy in key policy quarters – continues to colour dominant analyses with obstinacy, rehearsing the following three fallacies: (1) We do not know what Al Qaeda is, (2) Al Qaeda is made up of impoverished ragtags, alienated drifters merely channelling their free floating anger animated by homicidal animosity, and (3) Al Qaeda wants to destroy the Western world and its way of life. The logical conclusion of these three arguments is that (4) Al Qaeda's demands are unacceptable, since they are apocalyptic, nihilistic and irrational.

Irrationality

Whereas 'war is an organized group activity that includes organizations having dynamics of their own that do not lend themselves to explanations based upon individual human behaviour patterns',[6] Al Qaeda's struggle is often presented as lacking rationality and as grounded in the whims of one or two particular individuals, Osama Bin Laden and his acolyte, Ayman al Dhawahiri. Such explanation highlights mindless violence and attributes it to nihilism and the absence of modernity. Depicting Bin Laden and Al Dhawahiri as madmen bent on wreaking havoc, this perspective, in effect, strips the military campaign of an eminently political entity of any cogency painting it as a gratuitous enterprise.

One commentator argued that 'the attacks on New York and the Pentagon were unprovoked and had no specific objective. Rather, they were part of a general assault of Islamic extremists bent on destroying non-Islamic civilisations. As such, America's war with Al Qaeda is non-negotiable'.[7] For another: '[The enemy's] objective is not merely to murder as many [Americans] as possible and to conquer our land. Like the Nazis and Communists before him, he is dedicated to the destruction of everything good for which America stands'.[8] For one thing, Al Qaeda cannot conquer the United States, for another, 'far from being irrational, extremists may rationally calculate that their political ends require the disruption of normal politics, within whose constraints they are unlikely to be achieved. Nor should we necessarily think of extremists as temperamentally intolerant of other views'.[9]

Finally, the denial of the attackers' rationality is anchored centrally in the rejection of the 'equivalence of intentionality', something not lost on the attackers themselves. A Hizballah militant remarks:

> The Americans pretend not to understand the suicide bombers and consider them evil. But I am sure they do. As usual they are hypocrites. What is so strange about saying: 'I'd rather kill you on my own terms and kill myself with you rather than be led to my death like a sheep on your terms?' I know that the Americans fully understand this because this is exactly what they were celebrating about the guy who downed the Philadelphia flight on September 11.[10]

Fundamentalism

A second etiology of Al Qaeda's motives, which also presents modernity as anathema to the group, places emphasis on its religious discourse and depicts it as a fundamentalist cult. It argues that Al Qaeda is conducting an all-out religious war on the West, a sort of *bellum contra totum populum Christianum*, and that its jihad is aimed at the re-establishment of the Islamic Caliphate.

Not only must we question the widespread assumption that every political movement which speaks the language of religion is potentially terrorist,[11] but even so, in the case at hand, Al Qaeda's Islamist phraseology is indicative of its political philosophy and its sociocultural affiliation – not necessarily its immediate political aims.

The conflict between Al Qaeda and the United States is not about the protection of purity, nor is it conceived of primarily to advance religious interests. Undeniably, there is a radical religious dimension – somewhat mirrored on the American side as illustrated by the statements of the US Deputy Undersecretary of Defense, Lieutenant-General William Boykin, that 'the enemy is a spiritual enemy ... he's called the principality of darkness ... the enemy is a guy called Satan ... Why are terrorists out to destroy the United States? ... They're after us because we're a Christian nation'[12] – but that is merely the spiritual context.

Jihad, as it were, cannot be equated with the US-centric, Christianity-derivative term 'fundamentalism' coined in 1920 by the Reverend Curtis Lee Laws following the movement initiated by the Presbyterians of Princeton. Holy War – like the ancient Israelites' *Milchemet Mitzvah* – is a war waged by spiritual power or fought under the auspices of a spiritual power and for religious interests. Jihad is a doctrine of individual pietistic effort of which military action is only one possible (and secondary) manifestation. For all the easy parallels, crusade and jihad are, strictly speaking, not comparable.

The minimising and elimination of Al Qaeda's political discourse, in favour of overemphasised religious views, sidesteps the reasons at the core of the discord and disagreement. Al Qaeda's political goals must be distinguished clearly from the religious rhetoric the group uses, particularly so since Islam is a religion with neither clergy nor intercession (and therefore no intercessionary corps), only learned scholars respected for their knowledge (the *ulama*). Though there is a measure of merging the *corpus politicum* and *corpus mysticum* functions, neither Bin Laden (a political leader) nor al Dhawahiri (a strategic advisor) nor al Zarqawi (a general) nor yet again Atta (a commando officer) are religious leaders, nor do they claim to head a prelature. Although their political statements rely on *ijtihad* (legal interpretation of religious principles in light of changing historical contexts), as seen in Bin Laden's rationalisation of the targeting of civilians, theirs is a war committed to – 'offered' is the term of art – in the service of the Islamic nation (as a group of people) and its (historical) interests.

Hatred

A third group of analysts locates Al Qaeda's motivations in hatred harboured towards the West in general and the United States in particular. The subtext of this line of thinking is a plethora of analyses in recent years – from Bernard Lewis' celebrated 1990 essay on 'The Roots of Muslim Rage' to the 'Axis of Evil' phrase coined by Presidential speech-writer David Frum and made public by President George W. Bush in January 2002. The rationale, here, is that the feelings of hatred that allegedly motivate Al Qaeda's members and their supporters originate *ad hominem* in a miasma of personal humiliation, frustration and jealousy. The result is a clarion call for necessary actions against an 'evil' that hates democracy and the Western 'way of life'.

Christopher Hitchens' approach embodies this perspective. The journalist and political commentator writes:

Here was a direct, unmistakable confrontation between everything I loved and everything I hated. On one side, the ethics of the multicultural, the secular, the sceptical, and the cosmopolitan ... On the other, the arid monochrome of dull and vicious theocratic fascism. I am prepared for this war to go on for a very long time. I will never become tired of waging it, because it is a fight over essentials. And because it is so interesting.[13]

These three schools of thought on Al Qaeda betoken a static, monolithic view of the group. Yet as Chicago University's Robert Pape's research has demonstrated:

Few suicide attackers are social misfits, criminally insane, or professional losers ... The bottom line is that suicide terrorism is mainly a response to foreign occupation ... [It] is best understood as an extreme strategy for national liberation against democracies with troops that pose an imminent threat ... If suicide terrorism were mainly irrational or even disorganized, we would expect a much different pattern: political goals would not be articulated ... or the stated goals would vary considerably, even within the same conflict.[14]

Al Qaeda is neither conducting an apocalyptic, theological march on the 'civilized/free world' nor pursuing an obliterative war on democracy. In his 29 October 2004 message to the American people, Bin Laden indicated that President George W. Bush was wrong to 'claim that we hate freedom', adding: 'If so, then let him explain to us why we do not strike Sweden, for example'. The persistence of misconceptions (and the convenience of misrepresentation) constitutes a strategic consensus which rests, essentially, on unrealistic hopes of a medley of the enemy's eradication and ideological conversion. In the face of the sense of limitation represented by such solutionism and the increasing ambition of Al Qaeda – 'our conditions are always improving and becoming better, while your conditions are to the contrary of this', declared Bin Laden in January 2006 — the political reasons at the core of the group's assumption of a leading role in international affairs and its war-making capabilities must become the subject of scientific and sustained attention.

Perfunctorily presented, hence, the three constellations of explanations misassign the causes of the violence. They substitute psychological, theological and cultural reasons for political ones, and espouse platitudinous, unrelated ideas about the lack of democracy in the Arab world. Seeking an explanation for political violence in cultural terms is misleading. The war waged by Al Qaeda is done so for declared political goals.

THE PRIMACY OF THE POLITICAL

The domination of the various faulty explanations summarised above is particularly surprising in the face of non-ambiguous statements made by Al Qaeda as to the three main reasons for its war on the United States. These have been rehearsed consistently and regularly since 1996, notably in the August 1996 and February 1998 Declarations of War and the November 2002 and October 2004 justifications for its continuation.

Between the 11 September 2001 attacks on New York and Washington and mid-2006, Osama Bin Laden and Ayman al Dhawahiri have delivered, respectively, 23 messages each via audio or videotape in which a threefold case was reiterated, namely that the United States (1) ends its military presence in the Middle East, (2) ceases its uncritical political support of and military aid to Israel's illegal occupation of Palestinian territories, and (3) halts its support of corrupt and repressive illegitimate regimes in the Arab and Muslim world. To these accusations of direct and indirect occupation and of being an accessory to the fact of repression, Al Qaeda demands that, generally, the United States stops threatening the security of Muslims.

In the Declaration of War against the Americans Occupying the Land of the Two Holy Places of 23 August 1996, Al Qaeda indicated in relation to its reasons to resort to war:

We will list them, in order to remind everyone. First, for seven years [since the 1990 Gulf crisis], the United States has been *occupying* the lands of Islam in the holiest of places, the Arabian Peninsula, ... and turning its bases in the peninsula into a spearhead through which to fight the neighbouring Muslim peoples. Second, ... the great devastation inflicted on the Iraqi people ... with the protracted *blockade* imposed after the ... [1991 Gulf] war and the fragmentation and devastation. Third, ... the aim is also ... to divert attention from the *occupation* of Jerusalem ... All these crimes ... committed by the Americans are a clear declaration of war ... and scholars have throughout Islamic history agreed unanimously that the Jihad is an individual duty if the enemy destroys Muslim countries. (Emphasis added.)

Two years later, in the Declaration of War by Osama Bin Laden and the leaders of the World Islamic Front (*Al Jabha al Islamiya al 'Alamiya*) of 23 February 1998, it is noted similarly that:

For about seven years, the United States has been occupying the most sacred lands of Islam, *stealing* its *resources*, dictating to its rulers, humiliating its peoples, terrorizing its neighbours, and turning its bases in the peninsula into a spearhead through which to fight the neighbouring Muslim peoples ... Terrorizing you while you are carrying arms on our land is a *legitimate* and morally demanded duty. It is a *legitimate right*. (Emphasis added.)

Following the New York and Washington attacks and the inception of the conflict in Afghanistan, Bin Laden declared in a 6 November 2001 interview: 'If the Muslims do not have security, the Americans also will not have it. This is a very simple formula ... This is the formula of live and let live'.

A year later, on 12 November 2002, Bin Laden issued a message 'to the peoples of the countries who have entered into a coalition with the... American administration' where he articulated further such *lex talionis* and the reciprocity issue that stands at the heart of this conflict:

The road to safety begins with the removal of *aggression*, and justice stipulates exacting the *same treatment*. What happened since the attacks on New York and Washington and up until today, such as the killing of the Germans in Tunisia, the French in Karachi and the bombing of the French oil tanker in the Yemen, and the killing of the Marines in Kuwait, and the killing of the British and Australians in the explosions of Bali and the recent operation in Moscow, as well as some other operations here and there, is but a *reaction* and a *retaliation*, an eye for an eye ... If you have been aggrieved and appalled by the sight of your dead and the dead from among your allies, ... remember our dead ... So how

long should the killing, destruction, expulsion and the orphaning, and
widowing continue to be an exclusive occurrence upon us while peace,
security and happiness remains your exclusive monopoly ... This is an
unfair predicament. It is high time we become equal ... So *as you kill, you
shall be killed*, and as you bomb, you shall be bombed, and wait for what
brings calamity'. (Emphasis added.)

There is, as well, historical continuity in the threefold
argumentation. In a statement issued after the first World Trade
Center attack in 1993, Ramzi Youssef (nephew of Khaled Sheikh
Mohammad, planner of the 11 September 2001 operation)
stated: 'This action was done in response for the American
political, economic and military support to Israel, the state of
terrorism, and to the rest of the dictator countries in the region.
Our demands are: stop all military, economical, and political
aids to Israel, and do not interfere with any of the Middle East
countries' interior affairs'.[15]

Before his 11 September 2002 arrest in Karachi, Ramzi Ben
al Shaiba, a member of Mohammad Atta's group in Hamburg
(and possibly the original twentieth hijacker who may have
been replaced by Zacarias Moussaoui when he failed repeatedly
to enter the United States), gave an interview to Al Jazeera
investigative journalist Yosri Fouda in which he made it clear
that the US hegemony and its policies towards the Islamic
world were the key motive for the attacks on New York and
Washington. Ben al Shaiba provided Fouda with a copy of a
lengthy monograph entitled *The Reality of the New Crusaders'
War*, which he had written to explain the attackers' motivations,
and asked the journalist to translate the monograph into
English and deliver it to the Library of Congress.[16]

Finally, in a videotaped testament broadcast by Al Jazeera on
1 September 2005, Mohammad Siddique Khan, one of the four
perpetrators of the 7 July 2005 attacks on London, addressed
himself thus to the West:

I am going to keep this short and to the point, because it's been said
before by far more eloquent people than me. But our words have no
impact on you, therefore I am going to talk to you in a language that you

understand. Our words are dead until we give them life with our blood. I am sure by now the media has painted a suitable picture of me. This predictable propaganda machine will naturally try to put a spin on it to suit the government and scare the masses … I and thousands like me are forsaking everything for what we believe … Your democratically-elected governments perpetuate atrocities against my people and your support of them makes you responsible, just as I am directly responsible for protecting and avenging my Muslim brothers and sisters. Until we feel security, you will be our target. Until you stop the bombing, gassing, imprisonment and torture of my people, we will not stop this fight. *We are at war and I am a soldier.* Now you too will taste the reality of this situation. (Emphasis added.)

In this one statement, Khan sums up Al Qaeda's *casus belli* and *modus operandi*. Aware of the invisibilisation of their avowed reasons ('our words have no impact on you'), an independent group of individuals ('just as I am directly responsible') voluntarily targets civilians held accountable ('your support of them makes you responsible') for their governments' policies ('bombing, gassing, imprisonment and torture of my people') within a martial context ('we are at war and I am a soldier') with a view to achieving reciprocal treatment ('until we feel security, you will be our target').

THE PROBLEM OF TERRORISM

The materialisation of this thinking must be matched by appropriate analyses and understanding. Typically, it has not. As noted, the nature of Al Qaeda as a novel type of actor encompassing a political programme and conducting a military operation has not been grasped fully. Conversely, its political goals have been muted or attenuated and the group's impress limited to 'terrorism'.

For a number of years, a discipline of 'terrorology' has hence been constructed, whereby the notion of 'terrorism' is employed not in response to honest puzzlement about the real world, but rather in response to ideological pressures whose fundamental tenets are skilfully insinuated through selective focus, omission and biased description.[17]

Yet terrorism is but a tactical strategy designed to achieve a specific purpose. As one analyst writes:

> The term terrorism is widely misused. It is utilized in its generic sense as a form of shorthand by governments and the media, and is applied to a variety of acts and occurrences ... Terrorism, if nothing else, is violence or threats of violence, but it is not mindless violence, as some observers have charged. Usually, when employed in a political context, it represents a calculated series of actions designed to intimidate and sow fear throughout a target population in an effort to produce a pervasive atmosphere of insecurity, a widespread condition of anxiety. A terrorist campaign that causes a significant threshold of fear among the target population may achieve its aims. In some instances, terrorism is potentially a more effective, especially from a cost-benefit perspective, strategy than conventional or guerrilla warfare. Unlike other forms of warfare, however, the goal of terrorism is not to destroy the opposing side but instead to break its will.[18]

As such, terrorism is merely a particular way to employ force massively and represents consequently a form of war. From the Jewish Zealots (also known as *Sicarii*), to the Muslim Assassins (*Ismaili Hashishiyun*), to the French *Jacobins* (of Robespierre's 'La Grande Terreur'), to Russian anarchists (such as the anti-Czarist *Narodnaya Volya* group), Chinese revolutionaries, Algerian, Palestinian and Irish nationalists, and Armenian, Sri Lankan or Basque separatists, the fundamental subjectiveness associated with what may be best described as 'the use of force to advance a political cause which involves killing of civilians' has persisted internationally.

This central political component and the inherent subjectivity associated with terrorism have indeed led to a definitional paralysis, whereby the process of employment of force by sub-state groups to attain strategic and political goals is not regarded as a form of war. Yet 'if, indeed, a type of terrorism is war, then it follows that it, too, rests on the same immutable principles of war as do the more classical

manifestations of the phenomenon. This being the case, a type
of terrorism that qualifies as a form of war should – indeed *must*
– be treated as a form of war'.[19] George Abi-Saab summarises
the conundrum:

> All international efforts for decades, starting with the League of Nations
> and continuing in the United Nations, to draw a comprehensive
> convention against terrorism (but not specific acts of terrorism) have
> hitherto failed, absent a generally accepted and shared legal definition of
> what is terrorism, a terrorist act or a terrorist group. This is not because
> of any technical impossibility of formulating such a definition, but because
> of the lack of universal *opinio juris*, particularly about the ambit of the
> proposed crime *ratione personae*. Roughly speaking, the major powers
> insist on limiting the crime to private actors, excluding from it state
> actors; small powers on the contrary insist on including state actors,
> while some of them would like to exclude freedom fighters.[20]

Sean Anderson and Stephen Sloan add:

> [The] moralistic blanket condemnation of terrorism makes it difficult to
> arrive at any dispassionate objectivity in understanding terrorism, and
> even the attempt to study terrorism without immediate condemnation
> of it may be viewed as tacit acceptance of what is judged to be pernicious
> and reprehensible. The disturbing questions of morality are carried over
> into the equally heated debate over the nature of terrorism in which
> competing interpretations of what terrorism really is also complicate
> the debate on terrorism.[21]

The dominant parameters of this vexed issue reveal the
impossibility of an equal claim to the law of war. In that
sense,

> no amount of legal argument will persuade a combatant to respect
> the rules when he himself has been deprived of their protection ...
> This psychological impossibility is the consequence of a fundamental
> contradiction in terms of formal logic ... It is impossible to demand that
> an adversary respect the laws and customs of war while at the same
> time declaring that every one of its acts will be treated as a war crime

because of the mere fact that the act was carried out in the context of a war of aggression.[22]

Absent minimal progress towards the resolution of this compliance conundrum, the irrelevance of the laws of war to non-state armed groups will persist.

Moreover, terrorism is almost systematically political. Significant exceptions were the nineteenth-century Indian Thug sect, and, recently, the Japanese sect Aum Shinri Kyo (which carried out a poison gas attack in the Tokyo subway in March 1995). Reviewing the 315 worldwide terrorist attacks between 1980 and 2003 (95 per cent of which were 'part of organized, coherent campaigns'), Robert Pape concludes his research thus:

> The strategic logic of suicide terrorism is aimed at political coercion. The vast majority of suicide terrorist attacks are not isolated or random acts by individual fanatics, but rather occur in clusters as part of a larger campaign by an organized group to achieve a specific political goal. Moreover, the main goals of suicide terrorist groups are profoundly of this world. Suicide terrorist campaigns are primarily nationalistic, not religious, nor are they particularly Islamic ... [E]very group mounting a suicide campaign over the past two decades has had as a major objective – or as its central objective – coercing a foreign state that has military forces in what the terrorists see as their homeland to take those forces out... Even Al Qaeda fits this pattern ... [T]o ascribe Al Qaeda's suicide campaign to religion alone would not be accurate. The targets that Al Qaeda has attacked, and the strategic logic articulated by Osama Bin Laden to explain how suicide operations are expected to help achieve Al Qaeda's goals, both suggest that Al Qaeda's principal motive is to end foreign military occupation of the Arabian Peninsula and other Muslim regions ... The taproot of Al Qaeda's animosity to its enemies is what they do, not what they are.[23]

Ultimately, the word terrorism is useful as a scientific category only if – beyond all semantic positional warfare – it successfully locates what is specific to certain economies and strategies of political violence and not to others.[24] In the case at hand, such *differentia specifica* indicates that political terrorism has been pursued by Al Qaeda as a strategic reaction to the absence of military reciprocity in its war with the United States, as well as the asymmetrical evolution of methods of war-fighting. To ignore this latter dimension and the links between aim, capacity and means is to fail to realise that were Al Qaeda to match the capabilities of its opponents, it would, arguably, resort to conventional weaponry. Terrorism is to non-state armed groups what *raison d'état* is to states: a malleable, self-imposing justification used to enact a political ambition.

Being a combat technique, terrorism can at any given point in a political struggle be replaced by a more effective tool, including possibly a legitimate one (e.g., conventional weaponry targeting proportionally *bona fide* military objects). The logic of conscious resort to an extreme, high-cost strategy such as terrorism is best encapsulated in the dramatisation of an exchange between Algerian National Liberation Front (FLN, Front de Libération National) activist Larbi Ben M'Hidi and a French journalist in the 1965 film *The Battle of Algiers* by Gillo Pontecorvo. Asked whether it is not 'cowardly to use [w]omen's baskets to carry bombs, which have taken so many innocent lives', Ben M'Hidi retorts: 'Isn't it even more cowardly to attack defenceless villages with napalm bombs that kill many thousands of times more? Obviously, planes would make things easier for us. Give us your bombs and you can have our baskets'. In that sense, terrorism is presented as a last resort method forced upon combatants who, arguably, would forego it should they be able to fight symmetrically rather than asymmetrically.

This potential symmetry has remained a constant feature of state vs. non-state and may not be as elusive as expected generally. Today, Qaeda cells are no different in their organisation from secret Pentagon battlefield intelligence units. Both are clandestine teams using technology and scouting potential targets. Similarly, the mutation of the group's strategic thinking is akin to the military doctrine developed by the United States Army during the Vietnam war, particularly the Laos and

Cambodia campaigns, namely to compensate for the absence of ground forces by an aerial campaign of unprecedented intensity, without regard to collateral damage.

Equally in need of understanding is the reactive nature of Al Qaeda's struggle and the related transformation of a movement initially aimed at reforming a group of states. For it is less violence that ultimately characterises the group than the political content of its message and, as noted, how it has midwifed a new approach to displacing the state. In that respect, the original six-point programme of *Al Ikhwan al Muslimeen* (the Islamist Brotherhood), founded by Hassan al-Banna in March 1928 in Cairo, concerned the development of a welfare organisation with no interest in violence. Only after the failure of the Arab armies to stand up to Israel in 1948 did the society turn to armed struggle.

Similarly, the two main forces that would ultimately be fused to form Al Qaeda in the late 1980s – the variegated groups of Arabs that volunteered to help the Afghans against the Soviets and the Egyptian Islamist groups (in particular *Al Jama'at al Islamiya*) – were initially acting to fill a gap, namely the security of their fellow Muslims (domestically and abroad), which Arab and Muslim governments failed characteristically to address (except rhetorically, and, in some cases, financially). Ayman al Dhawahiri, for instance, is a follower of the teachings of Egyptian Islamist Sayyid al Qutb, who was of the view that, in the final analysis, only physical force would remove the political, social and economic obstacles to the establishment of an emancipated Islamic community. An ideologue of contemporary Islamist radicalism, Qutb had developed his ideas during a visit to the United States in the late 1940s.

Hence, Al Qaeda is taking in its hand not so much weapons and the recourse to violence, but the conduct of domestic and foreign policy. That its legitimation mode is religious, at a time when Islamist movements have been gaining the upper hand in the Arab and Muslim world marking the nadir of the timid regional democratisation experiments of the 1990s, has only made it easier to translate a political message in terms of local concerns. In that sense, Al Qaeda's struggle – tantamount to an affirmation that 'the colonialist understands nothing but force' – was historically inevitable and likely to have a profound imprint on the region's geopolitics in the coming decades.

5

The Way Forward

Know the enemy and know yourself; in a hundred battles you will never be in peril.

Sun Tzu, *The Art of War*

How will the war between Al Qaeda and America end? The outcome of the confrontation is unclear. What is certain is that neither side can defeat the other. The United States will not be able to overpower a diffuse, ever-mutating, organised international militancy movement, whose struggle enjoys the rearguard sympathy of large numbers of Muslims. Correspondingly, as a formidable enemy, Al Qaeda can score tactical victories on the United States and its allies but it cannot rout the world's sole superpower at a time when that superpower is mightier than ever in its history.

Wars end traditionally with the victory of one side, which manages to impose its will. Yet here, 'if, on the one hand, a sub-state group has no expectation of obtaining military superiority over its opponent and, on the other, a state or combination of states has little hope of ending enemy operations by demonstrating its superior force then how can the operations of either be assessed as proportionate to purely military goals, or not as the case may be?'[1] What is more, both sides have strategies designed for a lengthy conflict. The United States' *Joint Vision 2020*, released by the United States Department of Defense, which emphasises 'full spectrum dominance' over 'adaptive enemies', is mirrored by Al Qaeda's seven-phase strategy until 2020 allegedly articulated in the writings of Al Qaeda senior operative Sayf al Adl (Mohammad Ibrahim Makawi).[2]

Rehearsed regularly in pronouncements by its senior leadership, echoed by junior and operational staff, Al Qaeda's *casus belli* comes down to the following request made, in a May 1998 ABC interview with John Miller, by Osama Bin Laden to the American people: 'I ask the American people to force their government to give up anti-Muslim policies ... If [Western] people do not wish to be harmed inside their very own countries, they should seek to elect governments that are truly representative of them and that can protect their interests'. By 7 October 2001, the message aired by Al Jazeera had become thus: 'I have only a few words for America and its people: I swear by God Almighty Who raised the heavens without effort that neither America nor anyone who lives there will enjoy safety until safety becomes a reality for us living in Palestine and before all the infidel armies leave the land of Mohammad'. From thereon, in pronouncements and deeds, Bin Laden's Al Qaeda would be involved in the furtherance of a design aimed at putting pressure on Western governments by way of their populations.

ENDING THE DEADLOCK

The extent to which Al Qaeda can achieve its goal of getting the United States, under any administration, to alter the nature of its policies in the Middle East and towards Muslims in general, and the degree to which the United States can manage to have Al Qaeda cease its attacks on the United States and its allies constitute the mainstay of this political conflict. The nodal point is the following: is the United States prepared to rethink some of its foreign policy choices? Unambiguous indications are that it is not.

The 9/11 Commission concluded that '[Al Qaeda's] is not a position with which Americans can bargain or negotiate. With it, there is no common ground – not even respect for life – on which to begin a dialogue. It can only be destroyed or utterly isolated'.[3] Yet the 'terrorists should not be rewarded' mantra does not apply readily to the current situation. These terrorists are *de facto* combatants, and justice, rather than material reward (as in the case of mercenaries, contractors or criminals), is what they are after. Such a hortatory position is also akin to perpetuating imbalance within the conflict, namely that only one side can decide on the beginning, form and end of hostilities. Ultimately, the examination of grievances may become an unavoidable process – an option which responsible statesmanship and courageous leadership call for.

Can non-military, political engagement be considered? Besides lives and time, what would the belligerents gain through this notional transaction? What avenues can be legitimately and meaningfully explored? What can be accepted to resolve the conflict? There are, as it were, incentives and disincentives. Almost two decades ago, Martin Van Creveld wrote:

> If, as seems to be the case, th[e] state cannot defend itself effectively against internal or external low-intensity conflict, then clearly it does not have a future in front of it. If the state does take on such conflict in earnest then it will have to win quickly and decisively. Alternatively, the process of fighting itself will undermine the state's foundations – and indeed the fear of initiating this process has been a major factor behind the reluctance of many Western countries in particular to come to grips with terrorism. This is certainly not an imagined scenario; even today in many places around the world, the dice are on the table and the game is already under way [...] Over the last few decades, regular armed forces ... have repeatedly failed in numerous low-intensity conflicts where they seemed to hold all the cards. This should have caused politicians, the military, and their academic advisers to take a profound new look at the nature of war in our time; however, by and large no such attempt at re-evaluation was made. Held captive by the accepted strategic framework, time and again the losers explained away their defeat by citing mitigating factors.[4]

Historical precedents abound as to the inevitability of a political settlement to a conflict pitting state and non-state actors. During the 1950s and 1960s in Algeria, the FLN violently opposing French rule (through the use of indiscriminate urban bombing campaigns) was considered a terrorist organisation by French authorities and its eradication was pursued (including by way of torture, summary executions and mass repression) before a political settlement was reached between FLN representatives and French officials in Evian, France, in March 1962. In Northern Ireland, cost-ineffective heavy-handed approaches (including internment) were replaced in the mid-1980s with a change of tactics leading, in turn, to political initiatives. Indeed, the lesson of Britain's experience in Northern Ireland is that only by discriminate political reform can terrorists be demobilised.[5] Arguably, that evolution was also influenced by the sustained IRA campaign including its direct targeting of the British Prime Minister in Brighton on 12 October 1984.

An immediate precedent within the current war confirms this approach, namely Al Qaeda's attack on Spain in March 2004. In effect, reversal of a policy perceived as anti-Muslim led to cessation of hostilities on the part of Al Qaeda and a formal statement to that effect. Spaniards' removal of a government that was seen overwhelmingly as not acting as per their democratic choices and its replacement by a government that opted for more positive relations with the Arab and Muslim world prompted Al Qaeda to announce that it would stop actions against Spain. The popular pressure exerted in reaction to a major Al Qaeda attack was the decisive factor in that evolution.

This episode was followed immediately by an offer of truce to European countries as a whole on the condition that they pulled their troops from Iraq and ceased interfering in Muslims' affairs. The United Kingdom rejected the truce and was attacked 15 months later. Al Qaeda in Europe, which claimed to have conducted the 7 July 2005 operation in London (as the Abu Hafs al Masri Brigades), declared that it had done so 'as retaliation for the massacres which the British commit in Iraq and Afghanistan'.[6]

Equally, the issues have been disclosed by one of the parties and indications to the possibility of a settlement stated. Osama Bin Laden did so explicitly in October 2002 declaring, 'Whether America escalates or de-escalates this conflict, we will reply in kind', and even more so, on 19 January 2006, when Al Jazeera

aired a videotaped message in which he extended an offer of
truce to the United States in the following words:

> We do not object to a long-term truce with you on the basis of fair
> conditions that we respect ... In this truce, both parties will enjoy security
> and stability and we will [be able to] rebuild Iraq and Afghanistan, which
> were destroyed by the war. There is no shame in this solution other
> than preventing the flow of hundreds of billions to the influential people
> and war merchants in America.

The offer was immediately rejected by the White House Chief
of State who declared: 'We do not negotiate with terrorists.
We put them out of business',[7] a position confirmed by Vice-
President Dick Cheney shortly thereafter. Eleven days later,
Al Jazeera aired a videotaped message in which Ayman al
Dhawahiri stated: 'Osama Bin Laden offered you a decent
exit from your dilemma, but your leaders, who are keen to
accumulate wealth, insist on throwing you in battles'.

By the summer of 2006, it appeared that the window of
diplomatic overtures that had opened in 2004 with Bin Laden's
pre-US presidential elections message to the American people
urging them to consider the implications of their government
policies (a message in which he did not call for a boycott of
President Bush in favour of John Kerry) was closing. In a 23
April 2006 audiotaped message aired by Al Jazeera, Bin Laden
declared: 'The politicians of the West do not want dialogue
other than for the sake of dialogue to gain time. And they
do not want a truce unless it is from our side only'. Rather
suddenly, a discourse that had been crafted carefully to appear
constructive reverted to a harsher tone.

That renewed radicalisation was linked to the policies of the
Western governments but also to the alleged consent of their
populations, as Bin Laden remarked in the 23 April message:

> The war is a responsibility shared between the people and the governments.
> The war goes on and the people are renewing their allegiance to its rulers
> and masters. They send their sons to armies to fight us and they continue

their financial and moral support while our countries are burned and our houses are bombed and our people are killed and no one cares for us.

After several messages in which the leader of Al Qaeda was talking to Western populations (see Appendices), the man was now talking *of* these populations (arguably to his followers) and explicitly depicting them as jointly responsible of the ills visited upon the Muslim world by their governments.

In light of such resolve and strategic setbacks the United States encountered in their 'war on terror', the current US position may constitute a military and political dead end. A professor of defence analysis at the United States Naval Postgraduate School writes:

> Facing a chance of losing may encourage negotiations ... [This] suggests we face some important choices in the main battlefield in the war on terror. We must either start fighting in new ways against Al Qaeda or else commence some form of diplomatic negotiations with them. Perhaps we should do both at once. But we must do something ... [N]egotiation is more important with the networks because they are harder to fight for us. Doing battle with them requires inventing new tactics that radically differ from those we traditionally employ against national armies ... [W]e must accept that there might never be a treaty signed. But there could be a tacit agreement among the combatants, after which terrorist attacks almost entirely cease and US forces begin an exodus from Muslim countries. Both sides have been saying they want the latter anyway.[8]

The parties seem, however, to have entered the conflict with no clear avenues to conclusion with, as noted, long-term military strategies. Both sides are also stronger than they previously were. Within a few years, the United States has emerged as a fully-fledged global empire with an expanded presence in a larger number of countries. For its part, Al Qaeda has been scoring important tactical victories; it constitutes now the biggest threat to the United States and some European and Middle Eastern countries. Consequently, neither side is under particular pressure to end the conflict rapidly.

Similarly, painting it as a sort of inevitability, each camp appears determined to fight to the end. In his January 2006 message to the United States, Osama Bin Laden declared: 'We are a nation that does not tolerate injustice and seek revenge forever. Days and nights will not go by until we take revenge as we did on 11 September, God willing, and until your minds are exhausted and your lives become miserable and things turn [for the worse], which you detest'.

Thirteen days after this message, US Secretary of Defense Donald Rumsfeld delivered a speech before the National Press Club in Washington entitled 'The Long War', in which he remarked: 'The United States is a nation engaged in what will be a long war ... fading down over a sustained period of time ...

Table 5.1   Major Al Qaeda Operations Against the United States and Allies: 1995–2005

Date	Target and Location	Casualties
13 November 1995	US-operated Saudi National Guard Training Center, Riyadh, Saudi Arabia	Seven, including five American servicemen
25 June 1996	Khobar Towers, Dhahran, Saudi Arabia	19 American soldiers
7 August 1998	US Embassies in Nairobi, Kenya and Dar es Salaam, Tanzania	242 people
12 October 2000	USS Cole, off the coast of Aden, Yemen	17 American sailors
11 September 2001	World Trade Center in New York, Pentagon and White House/Capitol (failed) in Washington	3,000 people
12 October 2002	Night club in Bali, Indonesia	202 individuals, mostly Australian tourists
12 May 2003	Al Hamra residential complex, housing Americans and British staff, Riyadh, Saudi Arabia	39 individuals, including 12 US citizens
11 March 2004	Atocha, El Pozo, Alcalá de Henares and Santa Eugenia subway stations in Madrid	190 individuals
7 July 2005	Three subway stations and a double-decker bus, London	56 people

The only way that terrorists can win this struggle is if we lose our will and surrender the fight, or think it is not important enough, or in confusion or in disagreement among ourselves give them the time to regroup'. This perspective was fleshed out subsequently in the *National Security Strategy of the United States of America* released by the White House in March 2006.

REASSESSMENT AND RECOMPOSITION

The conflict opposing the United States and allies to the transnational, non-state armed group known as Al Qaeda remains problematic in manifold ways, highlighting a legal, scholarly and policy gap. No constructive international consensus exists on this foremost problem, which remains the province of retributional violence, military phraseology and Manichean talk. While war has been transforming, with Al Qaeda's emergence being part and parcel of that reshaping, international law has not been able to address fully the questions raised by this new type of conflict.

The combined effect of a changed context, a new actor and policies of exceptionalism has allowed for a curtailing of international law which is being rationalised by way of a political and legal discourse. In particular, the 'war on terrorism' – 'our war with terror begins with Al Qaeda, but it does not end ... until every terrorist group of global reach has been found, stopped and defeated' declared President George W. Bush in January 2002 – has been an inaccurate and misleading concept as no other group besides Al Qaeda has been targeted.

The policy debate – with a strong, ever-denied cultural subtext and multipurpose pejoratives about impermissible use of force on the part of a non-state actor targeting civilians and conducting a political war – has been distorted consciously by self-referential strategists that have tended to ignore the global dimension of the issues at play. Virus analogies, psychological profiles and law-enforcement approaches have led to conceptual and tactical impasses, while highlighting the need for a parsimonious approach on a topic where conjectures abound. A nation cannot choose its enemy, nor redefine it to fit partial purposes.

Internationalising the debate and taking full stock of the actual facts of the matter is an urgent necessity. Though dismissed widely, congruity may in fact be inevitable for the resolution of the conflict. Al Qaeda is 'an entirely rational enemy, motivated by causes just as dear as those that drive Americans. It is bent ...on defending its own liberties in its homelands; it is amply armed, and is equipped with a better understanding of the strategies of fourth-generation warfare than Americans yet possess'.[9]

Osama Bin Laden's plan vis-à-vis the United States was ambitious and it has been successful. It has, in particular, confirmed the principle that, based on their moral force, decentralised, weaker entities can match a stronger military power. In less than five years, Bin Laden has become the most powerful and the most respected Arab political figure, dwarfing the 22 Arab heads of state, now presenting himself as a meta-statesman in the Islamic world. Though there are religious and political dissentient views, no leading Muslim intellectual or scholar has denounced him. Yet Bin Laden's appeal is not religious and Al Qaeda's war agenda is eminently political and concerned with self-preservation.

Osama Bin Laden has wrestled an embryonic and local group of aging, if battle-tested, 'Arab Afghans', merged it with a younger generation of transnational fighters and transformed the whole into a full-blown, dynamic and technologically advanced organisation (Al Qaeda), before embracing the loosening and diffused expansion of this matured structure into an umbrella federation (Al Qaeda al Oum). This strategy has allowed the man to be ahead of its troops and of its enemies. As Victor Davis Hanson notes: 'Every army possesses men of daring, but few encourage initiative throughout the ranks, and welcome rather than fear innovation, so apprehensive are they that an army of independent-thinking soldiers in war just might prove the same as citizens in peace'.[10] This is precisely what Bin Laden has done by inviting shadowy regional leaders, such as Abu Musab al Zarqawi in Iraq and

Abdelaziz al Moqrin and Salah al Oofi in Saudi Arabia, to take matters into their own hands and operate semi-independently. In so doing, the man has already rendered his death or unlikely arrest (in January 2006 he swore never to be captured alive) almost a moot point.

History teaches that engagement with terrorists invariably requires addressing the issues raised, namely acknowledging the collective grievances in which they anchor their acts of force, depicted as political actions in response to specific issues. Regardless of bravado statements on the part of the parties involved, the inevitability of that process is always present. In Iraq, we witnessed, in 2004–6, reports of contacts between the Iraq insurgents and the US government, as well as expressions of interest in negotiation with the fighters on the part of the US-supported Iraqi authorities. In 2004, Bin Laden proposed a truce to Europe, which was rejected. In 2006, he extended an offer of truce to the United States, which refused it.

The sum total of the textual evidence and sober analysis is that Al Qaeda would conceivably cease hostilities against the United States, and indeed bring an end to the war it declared against that country in 1996 and in 1998, in return for some degree of satisfaction regarding its grievances. Absent such dynamic, the conflict will persist in its violent configuration and, for Al Qaeda, war (understood as resistance) may remain an ethical imperative, as stated by Osama Bin Laden in his October 2004 message to the American people: 'Is defending oneself and punishing the aggressor in kind, objectionable terrorism? If it is such, then it is unavoidable for us'. Determined words of a swimmer in the sea under the rain.

The proper prognosis – purposive rationality – must first be accepted before a corresponding prescription can be adapted to the conflict that pits Al Qaeda against the United States. The issue is not airport security, the demise of Ba'athi Iraq or Osama Bin Laden's fate but the place of America in the world. Without such understanding, the debate about the genesis of 11 September will remain self-serving. So far, the United States government has opted not to address the reasons raised by Al Qaeda as the core reasons for its war, has shunned and ridiculed any possibility of negotiations and taken battle to Islamic lands in Iraq, Afghanistan, Pakistan and Yemen. In November 2004, the majority of the American people elected to support these choices.

If, therefore, the stripped-down perception is that the United States has embarked on a crusade of sorts against Islam, then Americans must awaken to the fact that such a war can never be won. A country (of 280 million) cannot defeat a religion (of 1 billion and 300 million believers). In the case at hand, America is also pitting itself against traditional societal forces, at a time when these forces are stronger than ever in the Islamic world, and weaker than ever in the West. One does not bomb a (1,300 year old) tradition or a consciousness out of existence – or indeed colonise it to 'democratise' it. It is neither wise nor, as we have seen and will in all likelihood continue to witness, without deadly risk.

Yet the United States and some of its Western allies continue to fuel or condone injustice in the Middle East, rationalise it and depict those Muslims opposed vigorously to their designs as 'fundamentalists' (during the 1990s) or 'terrorists' (in the 2000s) – or both in the cases of Al Qaeda and Hamas. Because it is inherently chimerical, this approach is in fact dangerous. Indeed, 'it excoriates "the violence and the savagery of the fanatic". But it forgets that it can itself be a form of self-righteous fanaticism, because, so proud of its own form of enlightened advance, it imagines that other parts of the world can be wrenched from their own forms of life. The hypocrisy of this speech is to suppose that a superior morality is self-justifying'.[11] Whereas, it can be argued, President George W. Bush has been merely invoking fanaticism to combat what he describes as fanaticism. As John Gray notes,

> anyone who thinks that [the post-September 11] crisis is an opportunity to rebuild world order on a liberal universalist model has not understood it. The ideal of a universal civilisation is a recipe for unending conflict, and it is time it was given up. What is urgently needed is an attempt to work out terms of civilised coexistence among cultures and regimes that will always remain different.[12]

Respectful coexistence, not merely tolerance, for justice is born out of respect and empathy.

In the final analysis, given the country's might and its democratic ideals, only an honestly peaceful and consistently balanced policy is in America's self-interest. This is where the fault and the contradiction lie. Yet policy by emotion rather than reason is what has characterised consistently the United States' approach to the Arabo-Islamic world, while double standards have dominated US foreign policy in the Middle East for the past decades. That policy has oscillated between looking for a way out of 'the Mideast quagmire', and remaining committed to the interests of the predator – now making a call for mutual concessions, now endorsing Israeli occupation.

During the 1990s, analysts referred to the United States as a 'reluctant sheriff' and a 'lonely superpower'. Blinded by a false sense of global victory through culture and commerce, the United States sleepwalked through that decade of illusions, committing one injustice after another in the Middle East, until, for many of the disempowered and embittered in the world, America received its comeuppance – three times filled and running over. After decades of Sisyphean resignation to American domination, millions of anaesthetised Muslims then saw their eagerest hope come true. Earning its name, the 'Mother of all Battles' begat '9/11'.

What next then? Systematic terrorist campaigns vs. punitive world empires for the coming decades? Different degrees of deterioration or improvement can be envisaged. What appears certain is that the invisibilisation of Al Qaeda's *casus belli* serves no other purpose than perpetuating the safety of a faulty analysis. Spectatorship being here a recipe for victimhood, it is, therefore, imperative that the United States sheds the convenience of misrepresentation, and lives up to what in the end is no more than a challenge of responsibility. A week after the 11 September attacks, one analyst named and answered the dilemma for his fellow Americans: 'It is legitimate to ask whether shifting America's Mideast policy, in the aftermath of a horrific terrorist attack, would not signal to terrorists that they had won. The answer is no. After 11 September, doing the right thing has acquired a different urgency'.[13]

Reassessing and ultimately reorienting their foreign policy may indeed help Americans midwife a more secure future. In the final analysis, ignorance – even bias – is no absolution from responsibility. What that great responsibility spells out specifically is a willingness to understand the roots of the resentment directed towards America, and the will to act to remedy the injustice US policies perpetuate or generate. In so doing, the United States will live up to its self-proclaimed ideals.

Would that it were so. In the war that has opposed it to a transnational, armed Islamist group, the United States of America has suffered a threefold defeat at the hands of a dedicated enemy which managed adroitly to stalemate an asymmetrical conflict, of its own government who led it on a dangerous resumption of the Great Game in the Orient, and of its intellectuals who rhapsodised about just war rather than dissecting the science of *realpolitik*. Today, the country is at the crossroads, and the question is whether this past period of bad judgment, irresponsibility and hysteria has ushered a lasting phase, or whether it will be remembered as a time of overreaction to the 11 September 2001 attacks.

The 'war against terrorism' was in effect lost the moment it was decreed. As of now, with traditional allies alienated and those who followed fast retreating and Al Qaeda's tactical victories piling up, the United States is unambiguously perceived in Iraq and in Afghanistan as an illegitimate and brutal occupier rather than the benevolent liberator it insists on depicting itself as being.

Domestically, these conflicts came at a price of a partly manufactured permanent climate of fear and suspicion, an almost unprecedented loss of liberties, new entries in racial profiling and a Big Brother system of surveillance. It was the fog not of war but of self-delusion that paralysed this open society with Americans accepting that their government forbid them from merely seeing the 3,000 or so returning bodies of the soldiers it asked them to support in fighting an illegal, unjust and ill-conceived military campaign in Iraq. Internationally – from the coalition of the at-best-lukewarm to the forced grouping of the aggravated and unwilling – the path followed was self-destructive. In time, from Manila to Madrid, governments and citizens alike came to realise the consequences of the American folly in Mesopotamia.

The defeat was also that of American intellectuals who, with but a few exceptions, jockeyed for vengeful support of authoritarian and muscular policies aimed at countries that had not attacked them. Buttressed by the fallacy of neo-orientalist thinking, the inability of most to transcend Western eyes' perspective ensured equally that the words of Arabs and Muslims only be audible if they comforted dominant perceptions. The resulting depoliticisation of the conflict – whose stealth rationale is the dismissal of grievances and the avoidance of self-examination – was accomplished readily. It took three years for a leading local thinker to pose the question, 'Are we losing the war on terror?'. Writing anonymously, a seasoned intelligence officer tasked with fighting Al Qaeda answered: 'Bin Laden and Al Qaeda are winning'.

While on-the-ground professionals insisted that Osama Bin Laden is a CEO-styled, practical warrior concerned with forcing the United States to alter its policies vis-à-vis the Muslim world, American conservatives and liberals alike depicted ceaselessly the opponents of the United States as apocalyptic, envious nihilists. Such a climate of rationalisation of power and domination – 'for some countries some form of imperial governance, meaning a partial or complete suspension of their national sovereignty, might be better than full independence' suggested, in 2004, an acclaimed historian[14] – morphed with the rise of popular intolerance of 'others'.

This impossible stance in America went hand in hand with the instrumentalisation of the law, as a number of national legal commentators put forth the idea that, under special circumstances, torture – a most basic violation of international human rights law and international humanitarian law – could be administered. Though regrettable, they offered, 'torture works', and if a non-lethal dose of it can be used to save

(American) lives, it is a calculus worth making. Compliance with obligations made way for an unspoken yet palpable disdain for legalisms, which, it was argued, 'get in the way' of efficient combat. For violence-prone, transnational non-state actors, such as Al Qaeda-style armed groups, this translated into an invitation to have even less consideration for the rules of war. The distorted regimen in Guantanamo Bay was corrosive, and violations in Abu Ghraib begat violations of the beheading type.

Can the American defeat still lead to a victory? To be certain, abandoning the mindsets that have prevailed for the past years would, first and foremost, spell the death of specialised interests. Beyond, a society engulfed in excess and self-delusion cannot understand the simplicity of the war Al Qaeda is waging. Confronting the reasons behind the 11 September attacks risks robbing America of its victim status and uncovering the lack of correspondence between American ideals and US policies vis-à-vis Arabs and Muslims.

The coming decades may offer an opportunity for Americans to recompose their country, re-educate themselves about the pitfalls of sophisticated legal exceptionalism, stymie political bravado, and tackle foreign policy taboos. Alexis de Tocqueville once wrote that the privilege of America was to commit mistakes that could be corrected. Amid talk and practice of empire, whether that is still the case is, in the end, the burden of its citizenry.

Appendices

Between September 2001 and August 2006, the leaders of Al Qaeda, Osama Bin Laden and Ayman al Dhawahiri, released cumulatively 44 messages by audiotape or videotape. These communications have been either aired on the Doha-based, Arabic-language satellite news channel Al Jazeera (and in a few cases by their Dubai-based competitor Al Arabiya) or posted on short-lived Islamist websites.

The messages have generally had a lead theme: claim of a recent attack, commentary on international political affairs (in Iraq, Afghanistan, Pakistan, Palestine, Chechnya, the Sudan, Somalia and elsewhere), response to American or British allegations, and so forth. Often, the messages were also meant to serve as evidence of survival to attacks in the face of speculation, by the media or Western officials, that either man had been killed. A rough pattern emerged gradually whereby Bin Laden would deliver annual or semi-annual political overview messages and al Dhawahiri would issue statements every trimester or so, commenting more in detail on specific items in the news.

The intent seemed to be that, as leader, Bin Laden would cyclically reaffirm the purpose of Al Qaeda's campaign, speak to and of his combatants and address his enemies. Al Dhawahiri's interventions were more topical, almost managerial, and concerned with a variety of political issues constitutive of the wider context of Al Qaeda's war with its Western enemies. The appearances also served to reaffirm the men's leadership over the expanding and mutating organisation they created and sought to restructure in the wake of the US and British conquests of Afghanistan and Iraq.

The following four discourses by Osama Bin Laden are particularly important as they constitute direct messages, including two offers of truce, to the United States and European governments, and the American people. In these texts too, a recurring theme is noticeable: that of reciprocity. Time and again, the leader of Al Qaeda imparts that his group's struggle is driven by an inevitable *lex talionis*: 'Reciprocal treatment is part of justice', 'If you were distressed by the deaths of your men and the men of your allies ... remember our children who are killed', 'Just as you kill, you will be killed, just as you bomb, you will be bombed', 'Our actions are but a reaction to your acts', and 'Just as you lay waste to our nation, so we shall lay waste to yours'.

The translations from Arabic are based on English versions posted by Al Jazeera on its English-language website. The author has reviewed the original translations against the Arabic soundtracks aired by the channel, in a few cases amended the wording to clarify references and provided titles to identify what emerges as the lead theme in each intervention.

I
Message of Osama Bin Laden
to the Allies of the United States
'Just as You Kill, You Will Be Killed'
12 November 2002

In the name of God, the merciful, the compassionate, from the slave of God, Osama Bin Laden, to the peoples of the countries allied with the tyrannical United States government: May God's peace be upon those who follow the right path.

The road to safety begins by ending the aggression. Reciprocal treatment is part of justice.

The incidents that have taken place since the raids on New York and Washington up until now – like the killing of Germans in Tunisia and the French in Karachi, the bombing of the giant French tanker in Yemen, the killing of marines in Failaka [in Kuwait] and the British and Australians in the Bali explosions, the recent operation in Moscow and some operations here and there – are only reactions and reciprocal actions. These actions were carried out by the sons of Islam in defence of their religion and in response to the order of their God and prophet, may God's peace and blessings be upon him.

What [US President George W.] Bush, the pharaoh of this age, was doing in terms of killing our sons in Iraq, and what Israel, the United States' ally, was doing in terms of bombing houses that shelter old people, women and children with US-made aircraft in Palestine were sufficient to prompt the sane among your rulers to distance themselves from this criminal gang. Our kinsfolk in Palestine have been slain and severely tortured for nearly a century. If we defend our people in Palestine, the world becomes agitated and allies itself against Muslims, unjustly and falsely, under the pretence of fighting terrorism.

What do your governments want by allying themselves with the criminal gang in the White House against Muslims? Do your governments not know that the White House gangsters are the biggest butchers of this age? [US Defense Secretary Donald] Rumsfeld, the butcher of Vietnam, killed more than 2 million people, not to mention those he wounded. [US Vice-President Dick] Cheney and [US Secretary of State Colin] Powell killed and destroyed in Baghdad more than Hulegu of the Mongols.

What do your governments want from their alliance with America in attacking us in Afghanistan? I mention in particular Britain, France, Italy, Canada, Germany and Australia. We warned Australia before not to join in [the war] in Afghanistan, and [against] its despicable effort to separate East Timor. It ignored the warning until it woke up to the sounds of explosions in Bali. Its government falsely claimed that they [the Australians] were not targeted.

If you were distressed by the deaths of your men and the men of your allies in Tunisia, Karachi, Failaka, Bali and Amman, remember our children who are killed in Palestine and Iraq everyday, remember our deaths in Khost mosques and remember the premeditated killing of our people in weddings in Afghanistan. If you were distressed by the killing of your nationals in Moscow, remember ours in Chechnya.

Why should fear, killing, destruction, displacement, orphaning and widowing continue to be our lot, while security, stability and happiness be your lot? This is injustice. The time has come to settle accounts. Just as you kill, you will be killed. Just as you bomb, you will be bombed. And expect more that will further distress you.

The Islamic nation, thanks to God, has started to attack you at the hands of its beloved sons, who pledged to God to continue jihad, as long as they are alive, through words and weapons to establish right and expose falsehood.

In conclusion, I ask God to help us champion His religion and continue jihad for His sake until we meet Him while He is satisfied with us. And He can do so. Praise be to Almighty God.

2

Offer of Truce by Osama Bin Laden
to European Governments
'Reciprocal Treatment Is Part of Justice'
15 April 2004

Praise be to Almighty God. Peace and prayers be upon our Prophet Mohammad, his family and companions.

This is a message to our neighbours north of the Mediterranean, containing a peace proposal in response to the recent positive exchanges.

In my hands, there is a message to remind you that justice is a duty towards those whom you love and those whom you do not. And people's rights will not be harmed if the opponent speaks out about them. The greatest rule of safety is justice, and stopping injustice and aggression.

It was said: 'Oppression kills the oppressors and the hotbed of injustice is evil'. The situation in occupied Palestine is an example. What happened on 11 September and 11 March [the 2004 Madrid train bombings] is your goods returned to you.

It is known that security is a vital necessity for all human beings. We will not let you monopolise it for yourselves, just as vigilant people do not allow their politicians to tamper with their security.

Having said this, we would like to inform you that labelling us and our acts as terrorism is also a description of you and of your acts. Reaction comes at the same level as the original action. Our actions are but a reaction to your acts, which are represented by the destruction and killing of our kinsfolk in Afghanistan, Iraq and Palestine. The act that horrified the world – that is, the killing of the old, handicapped [Hamas spiritual leader] Sheikh Ahmed Yassin, may God have mercy on him – is sufficient evidence. We pledge to God that we will punish America for him, God willing.

Which religion considers your killed ones innocent and our killed ones worthless? And which principle considers your blood real blood and our blood water? Reciprocal treatment is part of justice and the one who starts injustice bears greater blame.

As for your politicians and those who have followed their path, who insist on ignoring the real problem of occupying the entirety of Palestine and exaggerate lies and falsification regarding our right in defence and resistance, they do not respect themselves. They also disdain the blood and minds of peoples. This is because their falsification increases the shedding of your blood instead of sparing it. Moreover, the examining of the developments that have been taking place, in terms of killings in our countries and your countries, will make clear an important fact: namely, that injustice is inflicted on us and on you by your politicians, who send your sons – although you are opposed to this – to our countries to kill and be killed. Therefore, it is in both sides' interest to curb the plans of those who shed the blood of peoples for their narrow personal interest and subservience to the White House gang.

The Zionist lobby is one of the most dangerous and most difficult figures of this group. God willing, we are determined to fight them.

We must take into consideration that this war brings billions of dollars in profit to the major companies, whether it be those that produce weapons or those that contribute to reconstruction, such as the Halliburton Company, and its subsidiaries.

Based on this, it is very clear who is benefiting from igniting this war and from the shedding of blood. It is the warlords, the bloodsuckers, who are steering world policy from behind a curtain. As for President [George W.] Bush, the leaders who are revolving in his orbit, the leading media companies and the United Nations, which makes laws for relations between the masters of veto and the slaves of the General Assembly, these are only some of the tools used to deceive and exploit peoples.

Based on the above, and in order to deny war merchants a chance and in response to the positive interaction shown by recent events and opinion polls, which indicate that most European peoples want peace, I ask honest people, especially ulamas, preachers and merchants, to form a permanent committee to enlighten European peoples of the justice of our causes, above all Palestine. They can make use of the huge potential of the media. The door of reconciliation is open for three months from the date of announcing this statement.

I also offer a peace proposal to them, whose essence is our commitment to stopping operations against every country that commits itself to not attacking Muslims or interfering in their affairs – including the US conspiracy on the greater Muslim world. This reconciliation can be renewed once the period signed by the first government [of the Western country] expires and a second government is formed with the consent of both parties. The reconciliation will start with the departure of its [the Western government's] last soldier from our country. The door of reconciliation is open for three months from the date of announcing this statement.

Whoever chooses war over peace will find us ready for the fight. Whoever chooses peace can see that we have responded positively. Therefore, stop spilling our blood in order to save yours. The solution to this equation, easy and difficult, lies in your hands. You know that things will only worsen the longer you take. If this happens, do not blame us – blame yourselves. A rational person does not relinquish his security, money and children to please the liar of the White House.

Had [George W. Bush] been truthful about his claim for peace, he would not describe the person who ripped open pregnant women in Sabra and Shatila and the destroyer of the capitulation process [Ariel Sharon] as a 'man of peace'. Reality proves our truthfulness and his [George W. Bush's] lie. He also would not have lied to people and said that we hate freedom and kill for the sake of killing. Reality proves our truthfulness and his lie.

The killing of the Russians was after their invasion of Afghanistan and Chechnya. The killing of Europeans was after their invasion of Iraq and Afghanistan. And the killing of Americans on that day in New York [11 September] was after their support of the Jews in Palestine and their invasion of the Arabian Peninsula. Also, killing them in Somalia was after their invasion of it in Operation Restore Hope. We made them leave without hope, praise be to God.

It is said that prevention is better than cure. Happy is he who has warned others. Heeding right is better than persisting in falsehood. Peace be upon those who follow true guidance.

3
Message of Osama Bin Laden
to the American People
'Your Security Is in Your Own Hands'
29 October 2004

People of America, this talk of mine is for you and concerns the ideal way to prevent another Manhattan, and deals with the war and its causes and results.

Before I begin, I say to you that security is an indispensable pillar of human life and that free men do not forfeit their security, contrary to [George W.] Bush's claim that we hate freedom. If so, then let him explain to us why we do not strike Sweden for example? And we know that freedom-haters do not possess defiant spirits like those of the 'nineteen' [11 September hijackers] – may God have mercy on them.

No, we fight because we are free men who do not sleep under oppression. We want to restore freedom to our nation. Just as you lay waste to our nation, so we shall lay waste to yours.

No one except a dumb thief plays with the security of others and then makes himself believe he will be secure. Whereas, when disaster strikes, thinking people make it their priority to look for its causes in order to prevent it from happening again.

But I am amazed at you. Even though we are in the fourth year after the events of 11 September, [George W.] Bush is still engaged in distortion, deception and hiding from you the real causes. And thus, the reasons are still there for a repeat of what occurred.

So I shall talk to you about the story behind those events and shall tell you truthfully about the moments in which the decision was taken, for you to consider.

I say to you, God knows that it had never occurred to us to strike the towers. But after it became unbearable and we witnessed the oppression and tyranny of the American/Israeli coalition against our people in Palestine and Lebanon, the idea came to my mind.

The events that affected my soul in a direct way started in 1982 when America permitted the Israelis to invade Lebanon and the American Sixth Fleet helped them in that. This bombardment began and many were killed and injured and others were terrorised and displaced.

I could not forget those moving scenes, blood and severed limbs, women and children sprawled everywhere. Houses destroyed along with their occupants and high rises demolished over their residents, rockets raining down on our home without mercy.

The situation was like a crocodile meeting a helpless child, powerless except for his screams. Does the crocodile understand a conversation that does not include a weapon? And the whole world saw and heard but did not respond.

In those difficult moments many hard-to-describe ideas bubbled in my soul, but in the end they produced an intense feeling of rejection of tyranny, and gave birth to a strong resolve to punish the oppressors.

And as I looked at those demolished towers in Lebanon, it entered my mind that we should punish the oppressor in kind and that we should destroy towers in America in order that they taste some of what we tasted and so that they be deterred from killing our women and children.

And that day, it was confirmed to me that oppression and the intentional killing of innocent women and children is a deliberate American policy. Destruction is [depicted as] freedom and democracy, while resistance is [presented as] terrorism and intolerance.

This means the oppressing and embargoing to death of millions as [George H.] Bush Sr. did in Iraq in the greatest mass slaughter of children humankind has ever known, and it means the throwing of millions of pounds of bombs and explosives at millions of children – also in Iraq – as [George W.] Bush Jr. did, in order to remove an old agent and replace him with a new puppet to assist in the pilfering of Iraq's oil and other outrages.

So with these images and their like as their background, the events of 11 September came as a reply to those great wrongs. Should a man be blamed for defending his sanctuary? Is defending oneself and punishing the aggressor in kind objectionable terrorism? If it is such, then it is unavoidable for us.

This is the message which I sought to communicate to you in word and deed, repeatedly, for years before 11 September. And you can read this, if you wish, in my interview with Scott [MacLeod] in *Time Magazine* in 1996, or with Peter Arnett on CNN in 1997, or my meeting with John Weiner in 1998. You can observe it practically, if you wish, in Kenya and Tanzania and in Aden. And you can read it in my interview with Abdul Bari Atwan, as well as my interviews with Robert Fisk.

The latter is one of your compatriots and co-religionists and I consider him to be neutral. So are the pretenders of freedom at the White House and the channels controlled by them able to run an interview with him? So that he may relay to the American people what he has understood from us to be the reasons for our fight against you?

If you were to avoid these reasons, you will have taken the correct path that will lead America to the security that it was in before 11 September. This concerned the causes of the war.

As for its results, they have been, by the grace of God, positive and enormous, and have, by all standards, exceeded all expectations. This is due to many factors, chief amongst them that we have found it difficult to deal with the Bush administration in light of the resemblance it bears to the regimes in our countries, half of which are ruled by the military and the other half of which are ruled by the sons of kings and presidents.

Our experience with them is lengthy, and both types are replete with those who are characterised by pride, arrogance, greed and misappropriation of wealth. This resemblance began after the visits of [George H.] Bush Sr. to the region.

At a time when some of our compatriots were dazzled by America and hoping that these visits would have an effect on our countries, all of a sudden he was affected by those monarchies and military regimes, and became envious of their remaining decades in their positions, to embezzle the public wealth of the nation without supervision or accounting.

So he took dictatorship and suppression of freedoms to his son and they named it the Patriot Act, under the pretence of fighting terrorism. In addition, [George H.] Bush sanctioned the installing of sons as state governors, and did not forget to import expertise in election fraud from the region's presidents to Florida to be made use of in moments of difficulty.

All that we have mentioned has made it easy for us to provoke and bait this administration. All that we have to do is to send two mujahideen to the furthest point East to raise a piece of cloth on which is written Al Qaeda, in order to make the generals race there to cause America to suffer human, economic and political losses without their achieving for it anything of note other than some benefits for their private companies.

This is in addition to our having experience in using guerrilla warfare and the war of attrition to fight tyrannical superpowers, as we, alongside the mujahideen, bled Russia for ten years, until it went bankrupt and was forced to withdraw in defeat. All praise is due to God. So we are continuing this policy in bleeding America to the point of bankruptcy. God willing, and nothing is too great for God.

That being said, those who say that Al Qaeda has won against the administration in the White House or that the administration has lost in this war have not been precise, because when one scrutinises the results, one cannot say that Al Qaeda is the sole factor in achieving those spectacular gains. Rather, the policy of the White House that demands the opening of war fronts to keep their various corporations busy – whether they be working in the field of arms or oil or reconstruction – has helped Al Qaeda to achieve these enormous results. And so it has appeared to some analysts and diplomats that the White House and us are playing as one team towards the economic goals of the United States, even if the intentions differ.

And it was to these sorts of notions and their like that the British diplomat and others were referring in their lectures at the Royal Institute of International Affairs when they pointed out that, for example, Al Qaeda spent 500,000 on the [11 September] event, while America, in the incident and its aftermath, lost – according to the lowest estimate – more than 500 billion dollars.

Meaning that every dollar of Al Qaeda defeated a million dollars by the permission of God, besides the loss of a huge number of jobs. As for the size of the economic deficit, it has reached record astronomical numbers estimated to total more than a trillion dollars.

And even more dangerous and bitter for America is that the mujahideen recently forced [George W.] Bush to resort to emergency funds to continue the fight in Afghanistan and Iraq, which is evidence of the success of the bleed-until-bankruptcy plan – with God's permission.

It is true that this shows that Al Qaeda has gained, but on the other hand, it shows that the Bush administration has also gained, something of which anyone who looks at the size of the contracts acquired by the shady Bush administration-linked mega-corporations, like Halliburton and its kind, will be convinced. And it all shows that the real loser is you.

It is the American people and their economy. For the record, we had agreed with the Commander-General Mohammad Atta,

God have mercy on him, that all the operations should be carried out within 20 minutes, before Bush and his administration noticed. It never occurred to us that the Commander-in-chief of the American armed forces would abandon 50,000 of his citizens in the twin towers to face those great horrors alone, the time when they most needed him.

But because it seemed to him that occupying himself by talking to the little girl about the goat and its butting ['My Pet Goat' children story] was more important than occupying himself with the planes and their butting of the skyscrapers. We were given three times the period required to execute the operations – all praise is due to God.

And it is no secret to you that the thinkers and perceptive ones from among the Americans warned Bush before the war and told him, 'All that you want for securing America and removing the weapons of mass destruction – assuming they exist – is available to you, and the nations of the world are with you in the inspections, and it is in the interest of America that it not be thrust into an unjustified war with an unknown outcome'. But the darkness of the black gold blurred his vision and insight, and he gave priority to private interests over the public interests of America.

So the war went ahead, the death toll rose, the American economy bled, and Bush became embroiled in the swamps of Iraq that threaten his future. He fits the saying, 'like the naughty she-goat who used her hoof to dig up a knife from under the earth'.

So I say to you, over 15,000 of our people have been killed and tens of thousands injured, while more than a thousand of you have been killed and more than 10,000 injured. And Bush's hands are stained with the blood of all those killed from both sides, all for the sake of oil and keeping their private companies in business.

Know that you are a nation who punishes the weak when he causes the killing of one of its citizens for money, while letting the powerful one get off when he causes the killing of more than one thousand of its sons, also for money.

And the same goes for your allies in Palestine. They terrorise the women and children, and kill and capture the men as they lie sleeping with their families on the mattresses. You may recall that for every action, there is a reaction.

Finally, it behooves you to reflect on the last wills and testaments of the thousands who left you on 11 September as they gestured in despair. They are important testaments, which should be studied and researched. Most significantly, I read some prose in their gestures before the collapse, where they say, 'How mistaken we were to have allowed the White House to implement its aggressive foreign policies against the weak without supervision'. It is as if they were telling you, the people of America, 'Hold to account those who have caused us to be killed, and happy is he who learns from others' mistakes'. And among that which I read in their gestures is a verse of poetry, 'Injustice chases its people, and how unhealthy the bed of tyranny'.

As has been said, 'An ounce of prevention is better than a pound of cure'. And know that it is better to return to the truth than persist in error, and that the wise man does not squander his security, wealth and children for the sake of the liar in the White House.

In conclusion, I tell you in truth that your security is not in the hands of [John] Kerry, nor [George W.] Bush, nor Al Qaeda. No. Your security is in your own hands. And every state that does not play with our security has automatically guaranteed its own security. And God is our Guardian and Helper, while you have no guardian or helper. All peace be upon he who follows the guidance.

4
Osama Bin Laden's Offer of Truce
to the American People
'We Have Already Answered You'
19 January 2006

My message to you is about the war in Iraq and Afghanistan and the way to end it. I had not intended to speak to you about this issue, because for us this issue is already decided on: diamonds cut diamonds.

Praise be to God. Our conditions are always improving and becoming better, while your conditions are to the contrary of this. However, what prompted me to speak are the repeated fallacies of your President [George W.] Bush in his comment on the outcome of the US opinion polls, which indicated that the overwhelming majority of you want the withdrawal of the forces from Iraq, but he objected to this desire and said that the withdrawal of troops would send a wrong message to the enemy.

Bush said: 'It is better to fight them on their ground than they fighting us on our ground'. In my response to these fallacies, I say: The war in Iraq is raging, and the operations in Afghanistan are on the rise in our favour, praise be to God. The Pentagon figures indicate the rise in the number of your dead and wounded, let alone the huge material losses and the collapse of the morale of the soldiers there as well as the increase in suicide cases among them.

Just imagine the state of psychological breakdown that afflicts the soldier while collecting the remnants of his comrades' dead bodies after they hit mines, which have torn them apart. Following such a situation, the soldier becomes caught between two fires. If he refuses to go out of his military barracks for patrols, he will face the penalties of the Vietnam butcher, and if he goes out, he will face the danger of mines. So, he is between two bitter situations, something which puts him under psychological pressure – fear, humiliation and coercion. Moreover, his people are careless about him. So, he has no choice but to commit suicide.

What you hear about him and his suicide is a strong message to you, which he wrote with his blood and soul while pain and bitterness consumed him so that you would save what you can save from this hell. However, the solution is in your hands if you care about your people.

The news of our brother mujahideen is different from what is published by the Pentagon. This news indicates that what is carried by the news media does not correspond with what is actually taking place on the ground. What increases doubts about the information of the White House's administration is its targeting of the news media that carry some facts about the real situation.

Documents have recently shown that the butcher of freedom in the world [US President Bush] had planned to bomb the head office of Al Jazeera Channel in the state of Qatar after he bombed its offices in Kabul and Baghdad, although, despite its defects, it [Al Jazeera] is one of our [Arab] creations.

Jihad is continuing, praise be to God, despite all the repressive measures the US army and its agents take to the point where there is no significant difference between these crimes and those of Saddam [Hussein]. These crimes include the raping of women and taking them hostage instead of their husbands. There is no power but in God. The torturing of men has reached the point of using chemical acids and electric drills in their joints. If they become desperate with them, they put the drill on their heads until death. If you like, read the human rights reports on the atrocities and crimes in the prisons of Abu Ghraib and Guantanamo.

I say that despite all the barbaric methods, they have failed to ease resistance, and the number of mujahideen, praise be to God, is increasing. In fact, reports indicate that the defeat and devastating failure of the ill-omened plan of the four – [George W.] Bush, [Dick] Cheney, [Donald] Rumsfeld and [Paul] Wolfowitz – and the unfolding and announcement of this defeat, is only a matter of time, which is to some extent linked to the awareness of the American people of the magnitude of this tragedy.

The wise ones know that Bush has no plan to achieve his alleged victory in Iraq. If you compare the small number of the dead when Bush made that false and stupid show-like announcement from an aircraft carrier at the end of the major operations, to the much greater number killed and injured in the subsequent minor operations, you will know the truth in what I am saying, and that Bush and his administration have neither the desire nor the will to withdraw from Iraq for their own dubious reasons.

To go back to where I started, I say that the results of the poll satisfy sane people and that Bush's objection to them is false. Reality testifies that the war against America and its allies has not remained confined to Iraq, as he claims. In fact, Iraq has become a point of attraction and recruitment of qualified resources.

On the other hand, the mujahideen, praise be to God, have managed to breach all the security measures adopted by the unjust nations of the coalition time and again. The evidence of this is the bombings you have seen in the capitals of the most important European countries of this aggressive coalition. As for the delay in carrying out similar operations in America, this was not due to failure to breach your security measures. Operations are under preparation, and you will see them on your own ground once they are finished, God willing.

Based on the above, we see that Bush's argument is false. However, the argument that he avoided, which is the substance of the results of opinion polls on withdrawing the troops, is that it is better not to fight the Muslims on their land and for Muslims not to fight the US on their land.

We do not object to a long-term truce with you on the basis of fair conditions that we respect. We are a nation for which God has disallowed treachery and lying. In this truce, both parties will enjoy security and stability and we will rebuild Iraq and Afghanistan, which were destroyed by the war. There is no shame in this solution other than preventing the flow of hundreds of billions to the influential people and war merchants in America, who supported Bush's election campaign with billions of dollars.

Hence, we can understand the insistence of Bush and his gang to continue the war. If you have a genuine will to achieve security and peace, we have already answered you. If Bush declines, and continues lying and practicing injustice [against us], it is useful for you to read the book *Rogue State* [by William Blum], the introduction of which reads: 'If I were a President, I would halt the operations against the United States'.

First, I will extend my apologies to the widows, orphans and the persons who were tortured. Afterwards, I will announce that the US interference in the world's countries has ended for ever. Finally, I would like to tell you that the war is for you or for us to win. If we win it, it means your defeat and disgrace forever as the wind blows in this direction with God's help. If you win it, you should read history. We are a nation that does not tolerate injustice and seeks revenge forever. Days and nights will not go by until we take revenge as we did on 11 September, God willing, and until your minds are exhausted and your lives become miserable and things turn [for the worse], which you detest. As for us, we do not have anything to lose. The swimmer in the sea does not fear rain. You have occupied our land, defiled our honour, violated our dignity, shed our blood, ransacked our money, demolished our houses, rendered us homeless and tampered with our security. We will treat you in the same way.

You tried to deny us decent life, but you cannot deny us a decent death. Refraining from performing jihad, which is sanctioned by our religion, is an appalling sin. The best way of death for us is under the shadows of swords.

Do not be deluded by your power and modern weapons. Although they win some battles, they lose the war. Patience and steadfastness are better than them. What is important is the outcome. We have been tolerant for ten years in fighting the Soviet Union with our few weapons and we managed to drain its economy. It became history, with God's help. You should learn lessons from that. We will remain patient in fighting you, God willing, until the one whose time has come dies first. We will not escape the fight as long as we hold our weapons in our hands. I swear to die only as a free man even if I taste the bitterness of death. I fear being humiliated or betrayed. Peace be upon those who follow guidance.

Chronology

2001

11 September: In an Al Qaeda-organised operation conducted by 19 kamikazes, two hijacked planes destroy New York's World Trade Center twin towers, and another plunges into the Pentagon. A fourth hijacked plane crashes in Pennsylvania. More than 3,000 people are killed.

7 October: The United States and the United Kingdom launch military operations in Afghanistan aimed at removing the Taliban from power. Al Jazeera airs a taped message by Osama Bin Laden: 'America will no longer be safe'.

2 December: A Sudanese national fires a Stinger missile at a US airplane inside the Prince Sultan airbase in Saudi Arabia.

22 December: A British national of Sri Lankan origin, Richard C. Reid, attempts to blow up American Airlines flight 63 from Paris to Miami, using C-4 explosives inserted in one of his shoes.

26 December: A new Bin Laden videotape is aired on Al Jazeera.

2002

28 March: Abu Zubayda, member of Al Qaeda and coordinator of the attacks on the US embassies in Nairobi and Dar es Salaam, is arrested in Faisalabad, Afghanistan.

11 April: A truck bomb attack is conducted by Tunisian Islamist Nizar Naouar against the Al Ghriba synagogue on the island of Jerba in Tunisia, killing 21 individuals including 14 German tourists.

8 May: In Karachi, Pakistan, a bomb explodes in front of the Sheraton Hotel killing 14 individuals, eleven of whom are French naval construction engineers.

14 June: A bomb explodes in front of the US consulate in Karachi killing twelve people and wounding 45.

5 July: An Egyptian national opens fire on the offices of the Israeli airline El Al at Los Angeles airport killing two individuals.

9 September: Al Jazeera airs a videotape in which Bin Laden details the 11 September operation and the identity of its 19 perpetrators.

11 September: Ramzi Ben el Shaiba is arrested in Karachi, Pakistan, along with eight Yemenis, a Saudi and an Egyptian.

6 October: A bomb attack takes place against a French oil tanker, the *Limburg*, near Sana'a, Yemen.

8 October: A group of American soldiers is attacked on the island of Failaka near Kuwait City, Kuwait. One US soldier is killed.

12 October: A bomb attack takes place at a nightclub in Bali, Indonesia, killing 202 people, mostly Australian tourists.

12 November: Bin Laden delivers an audio speech in which he declares to Western governments: 'As you kill, you shall be killed'.

21 November: In Kuwait City, a Kuwaiti policeman fires on two US soldiers gravely wounding them.

28 November: In Mombasa, Kenya, two SAM-7 missiles are fired on a Boeing 757 of the Israeli charter company Arkia. Almost simultaneously, a car bomb attack takes place outside the Paradise Hotel where several Israeli tourists reside. The attack kills 18 individuals including three Israelis.

30 December: Three US physicians are killed in Jibla, south of Sana'a in Yemen, by a Yemeni university student.

2003

(Attacks in Iraq are omitted.)

21 January: A US citizen is killed and another wounded during an ambush near Kuwait City.

1 March: Khaled Sheikh Mohammad, planner of the 11 September attacks, is arrested in Rawalpindi, near Islamabad, Pakistan.

20 March: The United States and the United Kingdom invade Iraq.

9 April: Baghdad falls to the US army.

12 May: In Riyadh, Saudi Arabia, the Al Hamra residential complex, housing Americans and Britons, is the target of three bomb attacks, which kill thirty-nine individuals including twelve US citizens; 149 are wounded.

16 May: In Casablanca, Morocco, 14 suicide bombers conduct five simultaneous attacks on the Belgian Consulate, the Spanish cultural centre (Casa de España), an Italian restaurant (housed in the Hotel Farah-Maghreb), and the Israeli Circle Alliance; 45 people are killed and 100 wounded.

5 August: A car bomb targets the Hotel Marriott in Jakarta, Indonesia, killing 15 and wounding 150.

8 November: In Riyadh, Saudi Arabia, a bomb attack targets a residential building housing foreign diplomats; 17 individuals are killed and 120 wounded.

15 November: In Istanbul, Turkey, a truck bomb attack takes place against two synagogues killing 24 and wounding 300.

20 November: Two car bombs target the British Consulate and the British bank HSBC in Istanbul; 27 people are killed and 400 wounded.

2004

11 March: Four simultaneous attacks, claimed by the European wing of Al Qaeda, take place in Madrid. Between 7:39 and 7:55 am, ten bombs planted in four different trains explode at the Atocha, El Pozo, Alcalá de Henares and Santa Eugenia stations killing 190 and wounding 1,434 individuals.

15 April: In an audio message aired by the Arabic satellite channels Al Arabiya and Al Jazeera, Bin Laden renews his commitment to fight the United States and offers to 'cease operations' against the European countries, which would stop 'aggressions against Muslims'. The truce proposal is rejected by European leaders.

1 May: An oil refinery in Yanbu, Saudi Arabia, is attacked by gunmen targeting senior executives at the facility, partly owned by Exxon Mobil. Five foreigners are killed, including two Americans.

29 May: In Khobar, Saudi Arabia, gunmen attack a building housing Western companies' offices killing 22 individuals.

18 June: A US engineer is abducted and beheaded in Jeddah, Saudi Arabia.

29 October: Al Jazeera airs a videotaped message from Bin Laden to the United States.

2005

7 July: Explosions take place in three underground trains and one double-decker bus in central London, killing 56 people and injuring 700.

23 July: Three bombs detonate in the Egyptian resort city of Sharm al-Sheikh, killing 63. Two of the bombs target resort hotels housing Western tourists and the third goes off in the city's marketplace.

19 August: Attackers fire Katushka rockets in the Jordanian port city of Aqaba, narrowly missing a US Navy ship, and killing a Jordanian security guard in a dockside warehouse. Two rockets are fired into the nearby Israeli port city of Eliat, causing minor damage.

1 October: Three suicide bombers strike tourist restaurants in Bali in Indonesia, killing 20.

9 November: On '11/9', three bomb attacks target three hotels in Amman housing Westerners, the Radisson SAS Hotel, the Days Inn Hotel and the Grand Hyatt, killing 76 and wounding 300.

29 December: The Iraqi branch of Al Qaeda fires rockets on Israel killing five soldiers.

2006

7 January: Al Jazeera airs a message by Ayman al Dhawahiri in which he claims that George W. Bush has lost the war in Iraq.

19 January: In an audiotape message aired by Al Jazeera, Osama Bin Laden offers a truce to the United States and threatens new attacks inside the United States.

30 January: Al Jazeera airs a video message by al Dhawahiri in which, referring to Bin Laden's January 19 statement, he declares: 'Osama Bin Laden offered you a decent exit from your dilemma but your leaders … insist on throwing you in battles'.

23 April: Al Jazeera airs an audio statement by Osama Bin Laden in which he renews allegations of complicity between Western peoples and their governments in their war against Islam and promises new attacks on Western countries.

25 April: Al Jazeera airs a half-hour videotape recording of Abu Mussab al Zarqawi, shown with his men in Iraq, in which he refers to the truce offer made by Bin Laden to the United States ('our leader Osama Ben Laden may Allah protect him, had offered you a long truce. It would have been better for you and those who are with you if you had accepted, but your arrogance pushed you to refuse').

28 April: Al Jazeera airs a videotape message by Ayman al Dhawahiri, originally posted on a website, in which he claims that Al Qaeda in Iraq has conducted 800 operations in three years and that this effort has 'broken the back of the United States' in Iraq.

24 May: Al Jazeera airs an audiotaped message by Bin Laden in which he declares that convicted 11 September 2001 plotter Zacarias Moussaoui has 'no connection whatsoever with the events of September 11th'.

8 June: Abu Musab al Zarqawi and several of his men are killed by a US airstrike on a house near Baquba, Iraq.

23 June: In a videotaped message aired by Al Jazeera, al Dhawahiri reiterates Bin Laden's statement that the United States will 'never dream of safety' until Palestine is free.

1 July: Al Jazeera airs an audiotaped message by Bin Laden in which he calls on Abu Hamza al Muhajir, al Zarqawi's replacement as head of Al Qaeda in Iraq, to pursue attacks on Americans.

12 July: The sixth Arab–Israeli war starts. It takes place between the state of Israel and the Lebanese non-state, armed group Hizballah.

27 July: Al Jazeera airs a videotaped message in which al Dhawahiri declares that Al Qaeda will not stand by while Lebanon and Palestine are attacked, and warns that: 'the entire world is an open battlefield for us, and since they are attacking us everywhere, we will attack everywhere'.

Notes

CHAPTER I

1. Francis Fukuyama, 'The End of History?', *The National Interest*, 16, Summer 1989, p. 9.
2. Samuel Huntington, *The Clash of Civilizations*, New York: Simon and Schuster, 1996, p. 217.
3. 'If that is the case', Frank Rich points out, 'history will have to explain why post-9/11 America was so quick to rein in the freedom of debate even as [Americans] paid constant self-congratulatory lip service to this moral distinction between them and us'. See Frank Rich, 'On "Fixed Ideas" Since September 11', *New York Review of Books*, 12 February 2003, p. 20.
4. For a fresh, sober and constructive analysis on this issue, see John J. Mearsheimer and Stephen Walt, 'The Israel Lobby and US Foreign Policy', Working Paper number RWP06–011, March 2006, John F. Kennedy School of Government, Harvard University.
5. Don DeLillo, 'In the Ruins of the Future', *Harper's Magazine*, December 2001, p. 34.
6. Edward Said, 'Suicidal Ignorance', *Al Ahram* (Cairo), 15–21 November 2001.
7. Michelle Malkin, *In Defense of Internment – The Case for Racial Profiling*, Washington, DC: Regnery, 2004, p. xxviii.
8. See Jonathan Alter, 'Time to Think about Torture as US Option', *Newsweek*, 5 November 2001; Alan M. Dershowitz, 'Is There a Torturous Road to Justice?', *Los Angeles Times*, 8 November 2001; and Bruce Hoffman, 'Should We Torture?', *The Atlantic Monthly*, 289, 1, January 2002, pp. 49–52.
9. Emmanuel Todd, *Après l'Empire – Essai sur la Décomposition du Système Américain*, Gallimard: Folio, 2002, p. 286.
10. Stephen Rosen notes: 'Writers from the political Left and Right ... not only discuss American imperialism but call for more of it in the name of humanitarian nation-building or global stability. Moreover, what is being discussed is not simply the reach and

influence of American capitalism or culture, but the harder kind of imperialism – the kind exercised by coercive intimidation and actual soldiers on the ground'. See Rosen, 'An Empire, If You Can Keep It', *The National Interest*, 71, Spring 2003, p. 51.

11. Norman Mailer, 'Only in America', *New York Review of Books*, 27 March 2003, pp. 49–53.

12. Anna Simons, 'The Death of Conquest', *The National Interest*, 71, Spring 2003, p. 41. In the early 1990s already, Paul Johnson was arguing that a number of countries could not govern themselves, and that 'civilized nations' would be forced to impose order where chaos was reigning. See Johnson, 'Colonialism's Back – And Not a Moment Too Soon', *New York Times Magazine*, 18 April 1993, p. 22.

13. For instance, Sam Harris, *The End of Faith – Religion, Terror and the Future of Reason*, New York: W.W. Norton and Company, 2004, depicts the tenets of Islam as enablers of terrorism.

14. The erroneous spelling of Dhawahiri's last name as 'Zawahiri' is due to the transliteration of a colloquial Egyptian pronounciation of the Arabic letter 'dha' as 'Za'.

15. The full texts of four of Osama Bin Laden's messages – 12 November 2002, 15 April 2004, 29 October 2004 and 19 January 2006 – can be found in the Appendices.

CHAPTER 2

1. Private correspondence, 23 May 1841. Cited in Olivier Le Cour Grandmaison, *Coloniser, Exterminer – Sur la Guerre et l'État Colonial*, Paris: Fayard, 2005.

2. Emran Qureshi and Michael Sells, eds, *The New Crusades – Constructing the Muslim Enemy*, New York: Columbia University Press, 2003, p. 11.

3. David Jablonsky, *Paradigm Lost? Transitions and the Search for a New World Order*, Westport, CT: Praeger, 1995, p. 55.

4. Sven Lindqvist, *Exterminate All the Brutes*, New York: New Press, 1996, p. 65.

5. Mahmood Mamdani, *Good Muslim, Bad Muslim – America, the Cold War and the Roots of Terror*, New York: Random House, 2004, p. 7.

6. Le Cour Grandmaison, *Coloniser, Exterminer*, p. 19. Also see Adam Hochschild, *King Leopold's Ghost*, New York: Mariner Books, 1999;

and Caroline Elkins, *Imperial Reckoning*, New York: Henry Holt and Company, 2005.

7. Heinrich Von Treitschke, *Politics*, Phoenix, AZ: Harbinger Books, 1963 [1897].

8. Le Cour Grandmaison, *Coloniser, Exterminer*, p. 20.

9. Victor Davis Hanson, *Carnage and Culture – Landmark Battles in the Rise of Western Power*, New York: Doubleday, 2001, p. 21. Also see Charles J. Dunlap, Jr, 'The End of Innocence: Rethinking Noncombatancy in the Post-Kosovo Era', *Strategic Review*, 28, 3, Summer 2000, pp. 9–17. Dunlap argues for a revisiting of the principle of distinction regarding military targets.

10. Cited in Jean-Luc Einaudi, *La Bataille de Paris*, Paris: Le Seuil, 1991, p. 48.

11. Jeremy Black, *War and the New Disorder in the 21st Century*, London: Continuum, 2004, p. 10. Black notes: 'Western warfare dominates general attention, leading to a failure to appreciate the diversity of conflict in the world, and its varied contexts, causes, courses, and consequences'.

12. Qiao Liang and Wang Xiangsui, *Unrestricted Warfare – Assumptions on War and Tactics in the Age of Globalization*, Beijing: PLA Literature and Arts Publishing House, 1999, pp. 4–5.

13. See Harlan K. Ullman and James P. Wade, *Shock and Awe – Achieving Rapid Dominance*, Washington, DC: National Defense University, December 1996.

14. Robert Montagne, *La Civilisation du Désert*, Paris: Hachette, 1947, p. 93.

15. Mary Kaldor, *New and Old Wars – Organized Violence in a Global Era*, Stanford, CA: Stanford University Press, 1999, pp. 4–5.

16. Didier Bigo, 'Nouveaux Regards sur les Conflits?', in Marie-Claude Smouts, ed., *Les Nouvelles Relations Internationales*, Paris: Presses de Sciences Po, 1998, pp. 330–2.

17. Herfried Münkler, *The New Wars*, London: Polity Press, 2005, pp. 107–8.

18. William S. Lind et al., 'The Changing Face of War: Into the Fourth Generation', *Marine Corps Gazette*, October 1989, p. 23.

19. Herfried Münkler, 'The Wars of the 21st Century', *International Review of the Red Cross*, 85, 849, March 2003, p. 9. Also see Montgomery C. Meigs, 'Unorthodox Thoughts about Asymmetric Warfare', *Parameters*, Summer 2003, pp. 5–18; and Stephen J.

Blank, 'Rethinking Asymmetric Threats', Strategic Studies Institute, Carlisle, Pennsylvania: US Army War College, September 2003.

20. Thomas Hobbes, *The Leviathan*, Indianapolis, IN: Hackett, 1994 [1651], p. 76.

21. Paul Gilbert, *New Terror, New Wars*, Washington, DC: Georgetown University Press, 2003, p. 10.

22. Gilbert, *New Terror, New Wars*, pp. 28–9 and p. 41.

23. Kaldor, *New and Old Wars*, p. 17.

24. Jean-Jacques Rousseau, *The Social Contract*, 1762, chapter 4.

25. Donald J. Hanle, *Terrorism: The Newest Face of Warfare*, London: Brassey's, 1989, p. 9.

26. Robert Kaplan, *Warrior Politics*, New York: Random House, 2002, p. 118. Also see Dan Belz, 'Is International Humanitarian Law Lapsing into Irrelevance in the War on International Terror?', *Theoretical Inquiries in Law*, 7, 1, December 2005, pp. 97–129.

27. Gilbert, *New Terror, New Wars*, p. 122.

28. Münkler, *The New Wars*, p. 61.

29. Faisal Devji, *Landscapes of the Jihad – Militancy, Morality, Modernity*, London: Hurst and Company, 2005, p. 63.

30. Karoline Postel-Vinay, 'La Transformation Spatiale des Relations Internationales', in Smouts, *Nouvelles Relations Internationales*, p. 167.

31. Hanle, *Terrorism*, p. 11.

32. Münkler, *The New Wars*, pp. 28–9.

33. Mamdani, *Good Muslim, Bad Muslim*, p. 222.

34. Cited in Hala Jaber, 'Inside the World of the Palestinian Suicide Bomber', *The Times* (London), 24 March 2002, p. 24.

35. Cited in John Alden Williams, ed., *Themes of Islamic Civilization*, Berkekey, CA: University of California Press, 1972, p. 262.

36. A transcript appears in Karen Greenberg, ed., *Al Qaeda Now – Understanding Today's Terrorists*, New York: Cambridge University Press, 2005, pp. 192–206.

37. Paul Gilbert, *Terrorism, Security, and Nationality – An Introduction Study in Applied Political Philosophy*, London: Routledge, 1994, p. 13.

CHAPTER 3

1. As early as 1981, it was emerging that the success or failure of Soviet activity in Afghanistan was contingent upon the extent of

external support for the mujahideen. See Alexandre Bennigsen, 'The Soviet Union and Muslim Guerrilla Wars, 1920–1981: Lessons for Afghanistan', N-1701/1, Santa Monica, California: Rand, August 1981.

2. Al Qaeda's name has purposefully a multilayered double-entendre. In Arabic, *qaeda* can mean 'precept', 'rule', 'norm', or 'column'. In a modern context, it also can refer to 'database' as in *sijil al qaeda* (database registry), another early reference to the organisation.

3. In 1998, as Bin Laden's popularity was gaining ground, the Saudi authorities reportedly offered to free his seized assets, double their amount and reinstate his citizenship on the condition that he praise King Fahd's religiosity. Around the same period, Bin Laden's mother, Aliya Ghanem, was flown to Afghanistan in a failed Saudi attempt to induce her son into renouncing his political ambition.

4. See Atwan's detailed account of his encounter with Bin Laden and informed analysis in Abdel Bari Atwan, *The Secret History of Al Qa'ida*, London: Saqi Books, 2006.

5. General J.H. Binford Peay III, US Central Command, Statement before the United States Senate Armed Services Committee, 9 July 1996.

6. *The 9/11 Commission Report – Final report of the National Commission on Terrorist Attacks Upon the United States*, New York: W.W. Norton, 2004, pp. 108 and 341.

7. Cited in Peter Bergen, *Holy War, Inc. – Inside the Secret World of Osama Bin Laden*, Carmichael, CA: Touchstone Books, 2001, pp. 19 and 21.

8. Cited in Steve Coll, *Ghost Wars – The Secret History of the CIA, Afghanistan, and Bin Laden, from the Soviet Invasion to September 10 2001*, New York: Penguin Press, 2004, p. 435.

9. See US District Court Southern District of New York, *United States of America v. Ali Mohammad*, New York, 20 October 2000.

10. Sun Tzu, *The Art of War*, London: Oxford University Press, 1971, p. 85. Martin Van Creveld, *The Transformation of War*, New York: Free Press, 1991, pp. 112–13. Also see his 'Power in War', *Theoretical Inquiries in Law*, 7, 1, December 2005, pp. 1–8.

11. Sheikh Nasser Ibn Hamid al Fahd, *Risalah fi Hukm Istikhdam Aslihat al Damar al Shamel did al Kuffar (A Treatise on the Legal Status of Using Weapons of Mass Destruction against Infidels)*, unpublished, 21 May 2003.

12. Devji, *Landscapes of the Jihad*, p. 53.
13. Van Creveld, *The Transformation of War*, p. 120.
14. Reuters, 'Iraq Al Qaeda Denies Blast that Killed Children', 14 July 2005.
15. Associated Press, 'Al Qaeda in Iraq Explains Jordan Bombings', 10 November 2005.
16. 'Tape Justifies Killing Innocent Muslims', CNN Arabic.com, 18 May 2005.

CHAPTER 4

1. Anonymous (Michael Scheuer), *Imperial Hubris – Why the West Is Losing the War on Terror*, Washington, DC: Brassey's, 2004, p. 223.
2. Karl Von Clausewitz, *On War* [Von Kriege], Princeton, NJ: Princeton University Press, 1976 [1832], p. 47.
3. Tomaž Mastnak, *Crusading Peace – Christiandom, the Muslim World, and Western Political Order*, Los Angeles: University of Los Angeles Press, 2002, p. 346. Mary Habeck remarks that 'of all the tomes on terrorism, Al Qaeda, Osama Ben Laden, radical Islam, the assault on America and the war on terror that have appeared in the past four years, only a few dozen merit serious consideration. The rest qualify as pulp non-fiction'. See 'Reading 9/11', *The American Interest* 1, 1, Autumn 2005, p. 101.
4. Michael Ignatieff, *The Lesser Evil*, Princeton, NJ: Princeton University Press, 2004, p. 23.
5. See Alan B. Krueger and Jitka Maleckova, 'Education, Poverty, Political Violence, and Terrorism: Is There a Causal Connection?,' National Bureau of Economic Research, Working Paper 9074, Cambridge, MA: NBER: July 2002; Office of the Prime Minister of the United Kingdom, *Responsibility for the Terrorist Atrocities in the United States on 11 September 2001: Britain's Case Against Bin Laden*, 4 October 2001.
6. Hanle, *Terrorism*, p. 3.
7. Richard Pipes, 'Give the Chechens a Land of Their Own', *New York Times*, 9 September 2004, p. A33.
8. Norman Podhoretz, 'World War IV: How it Started, What it Means, and Why We Have to Win', *Commentary*, September 2004, p. 18.

9. Gilbert, *New Terror, New Wars*, p. 85.

10. Quoted in Ghassan Hage, '"Comes a Time We Are All Enthusiasm": Understanding Palestinian Suicide Bombers in Times of Exighophobia', *Public Culture*, 15, 1, 2003, pp. 84–5.

11. Mamdani, *Good Muslim, Bad Muslim*, p. 37.

12. See Lisa Myers and NBC Team, 'Top Terrorist Hunter's Divisive Views', *NBC Nightly News*, 15 October 2003, www.msnbc.com/news/980764.asp?cp1=1#body.

13. Christopher Hitchens, 'It's a Good Time for War', *Boston Globe*, 8 September 2002.

14. Robert Pape, *Dying to Win – The Strategic Logic of Suicide Terrorism*, New York: Random House, 2005, p. 23 and p. 41.

15. Statement by J. Gilmore Childers and Henry J. DePippo before the United States Senate Judiciary Committee Subcommittee on Technology, Terrorism and Government Information Hearing on 'Foreign Terrorists in America: Five Years After the World Trade Center', 24 February 1998.

16. See Yosri Fouda and Nick Fielding, *Masterminds of Terror – The Truth Behind the Most Devastating Terrorist Attack the World Has Ever Seen*, London: Mainstream Publishing, 2003, pp. 196–202.

17. Alexander George, *Western State Terrorism*, London: Polity Press, 1991, pp. 92–3.

18. Neil Livingstone, *The War Against Terrorism*, Lexington, MA: Lexington Books, 1982, p. 4.

19. Hanle, *Terrorism*, p. xiii.

20. Georges Abi-Saab, 'There Is No Need to Reinvent the Law', *International Law Since September 11*, www.crimesofwar.org/sept-mag/sept-abi-printer.htm.

21. Sean Anderson and Stephen Sloan, *Historical Dictionary of Terrorism*, Lanham, MD: Scarecrow, 2002, p. 1.

22. François Bugnon, 'Just Wars, Wars of Aggression and International Humanitarian Law', *International Review of the Red Cross*, 847, 84, September 2002, p. 538. Indeed a senior commander of the Revolutionary Armed Forces of Colombia declared: 'It is supposed that for one to abide by the norms set forth in a pact, one should have participated in its drafting, in its discussion and should be in agreement with its conclusions'. See Daniel García-Peña Jaramillo, 'Humanitarian Protection in Non-International Conflicts: A Case Study of Colombia', paper presented at the International Institute of Humanitarian Law, San Remo, 2–4 December 1999, p. 8.

23. Robert Pape, *Dying to Win*, pp. 21 and 51.
24. Münkler, *The New Wars*, p. 99.

CHAPTER 5

1. Gilbert, *New Terror, New Wars*, p. 91.
2. See Bassam Badarin, 'Al Qaeda Has Drawn Up a Working Strategy Lasting Until 2020', *Al Qods al Arabi*, 11 March 2005.
3. *The 9/11 Commission Report*, p. 362.
4. Van Creveld, *The Transformation of War*, pp. 198 and 222.
5. Ivan Arreguín-Toft, 'Tunnel at the End of the Light: A Critique of US Counter-terrorist Grand Strategy', *Cambridge Review of International Affairs*, 15, 3, 2002, p. 559.
6. Statement posted on 7 July 2005 on www.qal3ati.com.
7. Scott McClellan, press briefing, 19 January 2006. Available at www.whitehouse.gov/news/releases/2006/01/20060119-.html.
8. John Arquilla, 'The Forever War', *San Francisco Chronicle*, 9 January 2005, p. C1.
9. Jonathan Raban, 'The Truth About Terrorism', *New York Review of Books*, 52, 1, 13 January 2005, p. 24.
10. Victor Davis Hanson, *Carnage and Culture*, p. 446.
11. Hywel Williams, 'The Danger of Liberal Imperialism', *Guardian*, 4 October 2001.
12. John Gray, 'Where There Is No Common Power', *New Stateman*, 24 September 2001.
13. Gary Kamiya, 'The Bloody Jordan River Now Flows Through America'. www.salon.com, 17 September 2001.
14. Niall Fergusson, *Colossus: The Price of America's Empire*, New York: Penguin, 2004, p. 170.

Bibliography

Abou El Fadl, Khaled. 'The Rules of Killing at War: An Inquiry into Classical Sources', *The Muslim World*, 59, 1999, pp. 144–9.

—— *Rebellion and Violence in Islamic Law*. New York: Cambridge University Press, 2001.

Abou Zahra, Mohammad. *The Concept of War in Islam (Nadhariyat al Harb fi al Islam)*. Cairo: Ministry of Waqf, 1961.

Aboul-Enein, Youssef H. and Sherifa Zuhur. 'Islamic Rulings on Warfare'. Strategic Studies Institute, Carlisle, Pennsylvania: US Army War College, October 2004.

Arreguín-Toft, Ivan. *How the Weak Win Wars – A Theory of Asymmetric Conflict*. New York: Cambridge University Press, 2005.

Atwan, Abdel Bari. *The Secret History of Al Qa'ida*. London: Saqi Books, 2006.

Bacevich, Andrew J. *American Empire – The Realities and Consequences of U.S. Diplomacy*. Cambridge, MA: Harvard University Press, 2002.

Bamford, James. *Body of Secrets*. New York: Anchor, 2002.

Barber, Benjamin R. *Fear's Empire – War, Terrorism and Democracy*. New York: W.W. Norton and Company, 2003.

Barnett, Roger. *Asymmetrical Warfare – Today's Challenges to US Military Might*. Washington, DC: Brassey's, 2003.

Bergen, Peter L. *Holy War, Inc. – Inside the Secret World of Osama bin Laden*. Carmichael, California: Touchstone Books, 2001.

Best, Geoffrey. *War and Law since 1945*. Oxford: Clarendon Press, 1994.

Beyerchen, Alan. 'Clausewitz, Nonlinearity, and the Unpredictability of War'. *International Security*, 17, 3, Winter 1992/1993, pp. 59–90.

Black, Jeremy. *War and the New Disorder in the 21st Century*. London: Continuum, 2004.

Blin, Arnaud. *Le Terrorisme*. Paris: Le Cavalier Bleu, 2005.

Bloom, Mia. *Dying to Kill*. New York: Columbia University Press, 2005.

Bovard, James. *Terrorism and Tyranny – Trampling Freedom, Justice and Peace to Rid the World of Evil*. London: IB Tauris, 2003.

Brown, Cynthia, ed. *Lost Liberties – Ashcroft and the Assault on Personal Freedom*. New York: New Press, 2003.

Browning, Peter. *The Changing Nature of Warfare – The Development of Land Warfare from 1792 to 1945*. Cambridge: Cambridge University Press, 2002.

Burgat, François. *L'Islamisme à l'Heure d'Al Qaida*. Paris: La Découverte, 2005.

Burke, Jason. *Al Qaeda: Casting a Shadow of Terror*. London: IB Tauris, 2003.

Chesterman, Simon, ed. *Civilians in War*. Boulder, CO: Lynne Rienner, 2001.

Cohn-Sherbok, Dan. *The Politics of Apocalypse*. Oxford: Oneworld Publications, 2006.

Coll, Steve. *Ghost Wars – The Secret History of the CIA, Afghanistan, and Bin Laden, from the Soviet Invasion to September 10, 2001*. New York: Penguin Press, 2004.

Contamine, Phillipe. *War in the Middle Ages*. Oxford: Blackwell, 1984.

Cooley, John. *Unholy Wars – Afghanistan, America and International Terrorism*. London: Pluto Press, 1999.

Devji, Faisal. *Landscapes of the Jihad – Militancy, Morality, Modernity*. London: Hurst and Company, 2005.

Dunlap, Jr., Charles J. 'The End of Innocence: Rethinking Noncombatancy in the Post-Kosovo Era'. *Strategic Review*, 28, 3, Summer 2000, pp. 9–17.

Einaudi, Jean-Luc. *La Bataille de Paris*. Paris: Le Seuil, 1991.

Esposito, John L. *Unholy War – Terror in the Name of Islam*. New York: Oxford University Press, 2002.

Fallaci, Orianna. *The Rage and the Pride*. New York: Rizzoli, 2002.

Fouda, Yosri and Nick Fielding. *Masterminds of Terror – The Truth Behind the Most Devastating Terrorist Attack the World Has Ever Seen*. London: Mainstream Publishing, 2003.

Fukuyama, Francis. *The End of History and the Last Man*. New York: Avon Books, 1992.

George, Alexander. *Western State Terrorism*. London: Polity Press, 1991.

Gerges, Fawaz A. *The Far Enemy – Why Jihad Went Global*. New York: Cambridge University Press, 2005.

Gertz, Bill. *Breakdown – How America's Intelligence Failures Led to September 11*. Washington, DC: Regnery Publishing, 2002.

Gilbert, Paul. *Terrorism, Security, and Nationality – An Introduction Study in Applied Political Philosophy*. London: Routledge, 1994.

—— *New Terror, New Wars*. Washington, DC: Georgetown University Press, 2003.

Gray, Colin S. 'Thinking Asymmetrically in Times of Terror', *Parameters*, Spring 2002, pp. 5–14.

—— *Another Bloody Century – The Future of Warfare*. London: Weidenfield and Nicolson, 2005.

Gray, John. *Al Qaeda and What It Means to Be Modern*. New York: Free Press, 2003.

Greenberg, Karen, ed. *Al Qaeda Now – Understanding Today's Terrorists*. New York: Cambridge University Press, 2005.

Gunaratna, Rohan. *Inside Al Qaeda – Global Network of Terror*. New York: Columbia University, 2002.

Habeck, Mary. *Knowing the Enemy – Jihadist Ideology and the War on Terror*. New Haven, CT: Yale University Press, 2006.

Hables Gray, Chris. *Post-Modern War – The New Politics of Conflicts*. London: Routledge, 1997.

Halliday, Fred. *Two Hours that Shook the World – September 11, 2001: Causes and Consequences*. London: IB Tauris, 2002.

Hanle, Donald J. *Terrorism: The Newest Face of Warfare*. London: Brassey's, 1989.

Hanson, Victor Davis. *Carnage and Culture – Landmark Battles in the Rise of Western Power*. New York: Vintage Books, 2001.

Harries, Owen. 'Suffer the Intellectuals', *The American Interest*, 1, 1 Autumn 2005.

Hashim, Ahmed S. *Insurgency and Counter-Insurgency in Iraq*. Ithaca, NY: Cornell University Press, 2005.

Hashmi, Sohail H. 'Interpreting the Islamic Ethics of War and Peace', *Journal of Lutheran Ethics*, 3, 2, February 2003.

Ian, Micah. *You Back the Attack, We'll Bomb Who We Want*. New York: Seven Stories, 2003.

Jablonsky, David. *Paradigm Lost? Transitions and the Search for a New World Order*. Westport, CT: Praeger, 1995.

Johnson, James Turner. *The Holy War Idea in Western and Islamic Traditions*. University Park, Pennsylvania: Pennsylvania State University Press, 1997.

—— and John Kelsay, eds. *Just War and Jihad – Historical and Theoretical Perspectives on War and Peace in Western and Islamic Traditions*. Westport, CT: Greenwood Press, 1991.

Jung, Dietrich, ed. *Shadow Globalization – Ethnic Conflicts and New Wars: A Political Economy of Intra-State War*. London: Routledge, 2003.

Kaldor, Mary. *New and Old Wars – Organized Violence in a Global Era*. Stanford, CA: Stanford University Press, 1999.

Keegan, John. *A History of Warfare*. London: Hutchinson, 1993.

Kepel, Gilles, ed. *Al Qaida dans le Texte*. Paris: Presses Universitaires de France, 2005.

Khadduri, Majid. *War and Peace in the Law of Islam*. Baltimore: John Hopkins Press, 1955.

Khaldun, Ibn. *The Muqaddimah – An Introduction to History*. Princeton, NJ: Princeton University Press, 1967 [1377].

Knox, MacGregor and Williamson Murray, eds. *The Dynamics of Military Revolution, 1300–2050*. Cambridge: Cambridge University Press, 2005.

Kolko, Gabriel. *A Century of War – Politics, Conflicts, and Society since 1914*. New York: New Press, 1994.

Krueger, Alan B. and Jitka Maleckova. 'Education, Poverty, Political Violence, and Terrorism: Is There a Causal Connection?', National Bureau of Economic Research, Working Paper 9074, Cambridge, MA: NBER, July 2002.

Laqueur, Walter. *No End to War – Terrorism in the Twenty-First Century*. London: Continuum, 2003.

Lawrence, Bruce. *Messages to the World – The Statements of Osama Bin Laden*. New York: Verso, 2005.

Lawrence, James. *The Savage Wars – British Campaigns in Africa, 1870–1920*. London: Robert Hale, 1985.

Le Cour Grandmaison, Olivier. *Coloniser, Exterminer – Sur la Guerre et l'État Colonial*. Paris: Fayard, 2005.

Liang, Qiao and Wang Xiangsui. *Unrestricted Warfare – Assumptions on War and Tactics in the Age of Globalization*. Beijing: PLA Literature Arts Publishing House, 1999.

Lindqvist, Sven. *Exterminate All the Brutes*. New York: New Press, 1996.

Livingstone, Neil. *The War Against Terrorism*. Lexington, MA: Lexington Books, 1982.

Lyon, David. *Surveillance after September 11*. Cambridge: Polity Press, 2003.

Mahmassani, Sobhi. 'The Principles of International Law in the Light of Islamic Doctrine'. *Recueil de Cours*, 117, The Hague: Academy of International Law, 1966, pp. 201–328.

Mamdani, Mahmood. *Good Muslim, Bad Muslim – America, the Cold War, and the Roots of Terror*. New York: Random House, 2004.

Mann, Michael. *Incoherent Empire*. New York: Verso, 2003.

Marks, Susan. *The Riddle of All Constitutions – International Law, Democracy, and the Critique of Ideology*. New York: Oxford University Press, 2003.

Mastnak, Tomaž. *Crusading Peace – Christendom, the Muslim World, and Western Political Order*. Los Angeles: University of Los Angeles Press, 2002.

McDermott, Terry. *Perfect Soldiers – The 9/11 Hijackers: Who They Were, Why They Did It*. New York: HarperCollins, 2005.

Mooers, Colin. *The New Imperialists – Ideologies of Empire*. Oxford: Oneworld Publications, 2006.

Münkler, Herfried. *The New Wars*. London: Polity Press, 2005.

Nabulsi, Karma. *Traditions of War – Occupation, Resistance, and the Law*. New York: Oxford University Press, 2000.

National Security Council (US). *National Strategy for Victory in Iraq*. Washington: National Security Council, November 2005.

Nye, Joseph S. *The Paradox of American Power – Why the World's Only Superpower Can't Go it Alone*. New York: Oxford University Press, 1992.

Olshansky, Barbara, ed. *Secret Trials and Executions – Military Tribunals and the Threat to Democracy*. New York: Seven Stories, 2002.

Pape, Robert A. *Dying to Win – The Strategic Logic of Suicide Terrorism*. New York: Random House, 2005.

Parenti, Christian. *The Soft Cage – Surveillance in America from Slavery to the War on Terror*. New York: Basic Books, 2003.

Phares, Walid. *Future Jihad – Terrorist Strategies Against America*. New York: Palgrave, Macmillan, 2005.

Ramsey, Paul. *The Just War – Force and Political Responsibility*. New York: Charles Scribner's Sons, 1968.

Said, Edward, W. *Orientalism*. New York: Pantheon Books, 1978.

Salamé, Ghassan. *Quand l'Amérique Refait le Monde*. Paris: Fayard, 2005.

Sandler, Todd, John T. Tschirhart, and Jon Cauley. 'A Theoretical Analysis of Transnational Terrorism', *The American Political Science Review*, 77, 1, March 1983, pp. 36–54.

Schmitt, Carl. *The Concept of the Political*. New Brunswick, NJ: Rutgers University Press, 1976.

Scruton, Roger. *The West and the Rest – Globalization and the Terrorist Threat.* Wilmington, DE: ISI Books, 2002.

Smith, Paul J. 'Transnational Terrorism and the Al Qaeda Model: Confronting New Realities', *Parameters*, Summer 2002, pp. 33–46.

Smith, Tom W., Kenneth A. Rasinski and Marianna Toce. *America Rebounds: A National Study of Public Response to the September 11 Terrorist Attacks.* Chicago: National Opinion Research Center, 2001.

Smouts, Marie-Claude, ed. *Les Nouvelles Relations Internationales – Pratiques et Théories.* Paris: Presses de Sciences Po, 1998.

Sun Tzu, *The Art of War.* London: Oxford University Press, 1971.

Todd, Emmanuel. *Après l'Empire – Essai sur la Décomposition du Système Américain.* Paris: Gallimard, 2002.

Van Creveld, Martin. *The Transformation of War.* New York: Free Press, 1991.

Volpi, Frederic, ed. *Transnational Islam and Regional Security.* New York: Routledge, 2006.

Von Clausewitz, Karl. *On War [Vom Kriege].* Princeton, NJ: Princeton University Press, 1976 [1832].

Wallerstein, Immanuel. *The Decline of American Power – The US in a Chaotic World.* New York: New Press, 2003.

Walzer, Michael. *Just and Unjust Wars – A Moral Argument with Historical Illustrations*, third edition. New York: Basic Books, 2000.

Wesseling, Henk L. *Imperialism and War – Essays on Colonial Wars in Asia and Africa.* Leyde: Brill, 1989.

White House *The National Security Strategy of the United States of America.* Washington: White House, September 2002.

—— *The National Security Strategy of the United States of America.* Washington: White House, March 2006.

Wippman, David and Matthew Evangelista, eds. *New Wars, New Laws? – Applying the Laws of War and 21st Century Conflicts.* Ardsley, NY: Transnational Publishers, 2005.

Index